D0583641

CALGARY PUBLIC LIBRARY

AUG   2012

SOLID CONTACT

SOLID
CONTACT

A Top Golf Instructor's Guide to
Learning Your Swing DNA and Instantly
Striking the Ball Better Than Ever

JIM HARDY

with RON KASPRISKE

GOTHAM
BOOKS

GOTHAM BOOKS
Published by Penguin Group (USA) Inc.
375 Hudson Street, New York, New York 10014, U.S.A.
Penguin Group (Canada), 90 Eglinton Avenue East, Suite 700, Toronto, Ontario M4P 2Y3,
Canada (a division of Pearson Penguin Canada Inc.); Penguin Books Ltd, 80 Strand, London
WC2R 0RL, England; Penguin Ireland, 25 St. Stephen's Green, Dublin 2, Ireland (a division
of Penguin Books Ltd); Penguin Group (Australia), 250 Camberwell Road, Camberwell,
Victoria 3124, Australia (a division of Pearson Australia Group Pty Ltd); Penguin Books
India Pvt Ltd, 11 Community Centre, Panchsheel Park, New Delhi – 110 017, India; Penguin
Group (NZ), 67 Apollo Drive, Rosedale, Auckland 0632, New Zealand (a division of Pearson
New Zealand Ltd); Penguin Books (South Africa) (Pty) Ltd, 24 Sturdee Avenue, Rosebank,
Johannesburg 2196, South Africa

Penguin Books Ltd, Registered Offices: 80 Strand, London WC2R 0RL, England

Published by Gotham Books, a member of Penguin Group (USA) Inc.

First printing, March 2012

10 9 8 7 6 5 4 3 2 1

Copyright © 2012 by Jim Hardy

Illustrations by Scott Addison
All rights reserved

Gotham Books and the skyscraper logo are trademarks of Penguin Group (USA) Inc.

LIBRARY OF CONGRESS CATALOGING-IN-PUBLICATION DATA

Hardy, Jim.
    Solid contact : a top golf instructor's guide to learning your swing DNA and instantly strik-
ing the ball better than ever / Jim Hardy with Ron Kaspriske.
        p. cm.
    ISBN 978-1-59240-658-6 (hardback)
    1. Swing (Golf)—Handbooks, manuals, etc.   2. Golf—Training—Handbooks, manuals, etc.
I. Kaspriske, Ron.   II. Title.
    GV979.S9H295 2012
    796.352'3—dc23   2011046703

Printed in the United States of America

Set in New Aster and Din Schrift
Designed by BTD NYC

Without limiting the rights under copyright reserved above, no part of this publication may
be reproduced, stored in or introduced into a retrieval system, or transmitted, in any form,
or by any means (electronic, mechanical, photocopying, recording, or otherwise), without
the prior written permission of both the copyright owner and the above publisher of this
book.

The scanning, uploading, and distribution of this book via the Internet or via any other
means without the permission of the publisher is illegal and punishable by law. Please pur-
chase only authorized electronic editions, and do not participate in or encourage electronic
piracy of copyrighted materials. Your support of the authors' rights is appreciated.

While the authors have made every effort to provide accurate telephone numbers and Internet addresses at the time of publication, neither the publisher nor the authors assume any
responsibility for errors, or for changes that occur after publication. Further, the publisher
does not have any control over and does not assume any responsibility for author or third-
party websites or their content.

I dedicate this book to Chris O'Connell and Mike Crisanti, whose enthusiasm and hard work have built Plane Truth Golf; to the Colonel and Bobby Thieme, who taught me the plain Truth that changed my life; and to Him in his matchless grace

CONTENTS

FOREWORD

BY MATT KUCHAR

Five swings. That's what it took for me to become one of the most consistent players on the PGA Tour. That might sound like hyperbole, but trust me, I'm not exaggerating. You hear professionals routinely say they're working on a swing change, and it might take months—or even a year— before they start seeing positive results from those changes. That wasn't the case for me. It took me exactly five swings. How's that possible? I was introduced to the teachings of Jim Hardy through one of his friends, a great instructor in his own right by the name of Chris O'Connell. Jim and Chris are partners in golf instruction, and the philosophy that Jim is going to teach you in this book is the very philosophy that Chris used to turn my career around.

Before I started working with Chris and learned what Jim's philosophy was all about, you could say, at best, I was a streaky player. I would find myself in contention to win a PGA Tour event a couple of times a year, but only when I was really timing my old swing well. Now I find myself among the top players on the PGA Tour nearly every time I tee it up. I always feel like I have a chance. During one stretch, I had nineteen top-10 finishes in forty-one events and I also led the PGA Tour in earnings in 2010 with $4.9 million. I owe it all to working with Chris and understanding Jim's plus/minus system.

Unlike things other instructors have told me and lessons I have taken, this concept just makes sense to me. I'm no longer bogged down thinking about swing mechanics. I just pay attention to my ball flight. If things go bad, I know I'm only one adjustment away from correcting whatever issue I'm having. If my swing is too steep or too shallow, I know all I have to do is add an ingredient from the other side of neutral and things will balance out. It's a matter of correcting one angle. A lot of people think you have to make several adjustments to start hitting the ball solid again. That's not true. In many cases, all you need to do is adjust one thing.

The best part about it is that I'm able to fix myself when things go bad. Chris can help me on the lesson tee, but if I start hitting it squirrelly during a tournament, I understand the reason for the misses and what to do to correct them. I think that's a huge reason for my consistency. I know I'm never that far off from making solid contact again and controlling my shots. To think you can self-diagnose your problem and quickly correct it. Man, that's pretty exciting.

The other thing I really like about this concept is that it de-emphasizes the notion that you have to make a perfect-looking golf swing to play great golf. It's not about the swing. It's about the result. Jim is saying that making solid contact with the ball, and playing a ball flight that you can rely on, is way more important than having a pretty swing. And I agree. I know a lot of amateur players who don't have the time or ability to make a great swing. They just want to go out and play golf and have fun. They know their swings will never look like they play on the PGA Tour, they just want to hit the ball solidly and have some confidence about where the golf ball is gonna go. This book will show you exactly how to do that. If you understand the concept, you're going to be on your way to playing better. And who knows, maybe it will only take you four swings to do it.

YOUR GOLF DNA

I f you've read my books and magazine articles, or listened to my lectures, then you're probably aware that I believe all golfers make either a one-plane or two-plane swing. What that means is, if the body, arms, and club move together on roughly the same plane, it's a one-plane swing. If the arms and club move on a distinctly different, more upright plane than the body, it's a two-plane swing. It doesn't matter whether I'm talking about a 20-handicapper or a tour pro—you're either a one-planer or a two-planer.

I bring this up because, in the past, I've taught what I felt were the easiest, quickest, safest, and best ways to produce a one- or two-plane swing. But the elements I taught for those one- or two-plane swings had a lot of latitude within them. Those latitudes allowed for individual swing variations. No two people are going to swing the club exactly alike. Each of us has our own physical limitations, strength, and flexibility. We have our own tempos, rhythms, and balance. We don't stand exactly the same, or aim the same, or have identical planes or paths. And each of us has our own style of one- or two-plane swing—and a great deal of them are very effective.

Let me give you a couple of examples of what I mean by "effective." Legendary golfers Jack Nicklaus and Tom Watson are both "two-planers," but their swings have never looked alike. The same is true of their ball flights. In their primes, Jack relied on a high fade while Tom preferred a high draw. Meanwhile, two more golf legends, Lee Trevino and Gary Player, swung the club as "one-planers." But guess what? They also had different-looking one-plane swings. Lee loved a low fade and Gary made a career out of playing a low hook. So if all four of these golf greats had different-looking swings and different ball flights, how in the world did they each win so many tournaments? The answer is simple—their swings were effective. They all hit the ball solidly with a consistent, predictable flight.

That's really the key to great golf. It's something my old friend John Jacobs, one of the greatest golf instructors ever, figured out years ago when he said that the sole purpose of the golf swing is to produce a correct, repetitive impact. The method employed is of no significance. I couldn't agree more. In the thirty-five years I've been teaching golf, I've had the opportunity to see a lot of different one- and two-plane swings that produced a "correct, repetitive impact." And while it sure is nice to have a beautiful golf swing, I don't know any great players who wouldn't trade it in a second for a swing that allowed them to nearly always hit the ball flush with a consistent shot shape. What good is a pretty swing if it doesn't hold up under the pressure of a Sunday at Augusta, or, perhaps in your case, during a Saturday morning Nassau? That's why I wanted to write this book. I want you to know that you can swing the club with the classic one- or two-plane form that I demonstrated in my previous books or in a one- or two-plane variation that works for you—as long as it's effective. The only thing that matters is that your swing produces solid impact and a ball flight you can count on. And I'm going to help you learn how to do that.

As I said earlier, no two golf swings are exactly alike. Think of them as DNA strands. I've got one. You've got one. Tiger Woods has one. You might have a swing that's similar to your favorite tour pro's swing, but there's always going to be one or two things that make it unique. That's why the adjustments you might need to improve your swing might not necessarily work for the guy next to you on the driving range—even if, to the naked eye, your swings look a lot alike. Please remember that. After decades of helping golfers and studying swing theories, I really believe instruction should always be tailored to an individual's needs rather than try to force a golfer to learn a rigid swing theory. As I said, all swings fall into two general categories (one-plane or two-plane), but there are countless ways within those two categories to produce solid and repetitive impact. Knowing that, does it make any sense to force a specific, no-latitude swing method on you? If we all decided that only Jack Nicklaus swung the club correctly, how could we explain all those trophies that Lee Trevino, Gary Player, and Tom Watson won?

In the past, if you wanted to get customized instruction to improve, it almost always meant hiring a golf instructor. But now, with the help of this book, I'm going to teach you how to diagnose what's going on with your own swing, and then I'm going to show you how to apply that knowledge to hit better shots. You won't need a second pair of eyes watching you, and you won't have to get your swing videotaped to figure out what's going on. You're going to be able to identify your swing's DNA by paying attention to your ball flight and the ground at impact, and then referring to charts in this book that will give you options for adjustments you can make to improve your swing. I'll walk you through how to do this later, but for now, you should be happy to know that you won't have to lock in to one solution. If one adjustment doesn't quite click for you, you can try something else from several lists of swing elements that are provided in this book. Remember, no two golfers swing exactly alike, so the solution to fixing your bad shots might differ from what works for the next guy. If you and your buddy are hungry and want to eat dinner, steak might be your choice, while he might go with fish. They both solve the problem of curbing hunger, but the solutions are a matter of personal preference. So when you use the charts in this book, you can keep trying things until you find the magic formula that helps you hit the ball more solidly with a repeatable ball flight. And I'm not talking about years, months, or even weeks of experimenting to improve. I don't say this lightly: With this book, you'll have the opportunity to be a better golfer on your very next shot! PGA Tour pro Matt Kuchar, who is a student of my colleague Chris O'Connell, said in this book's foreword that it took him "exactly five swings" to fix his swing, which led him to become the leading money winner on the PGA Tour in 2010.

The thing that makes this possible is my new, revolutionary system, which categorizes all the elements of your swing, the ground on which your ball was resting, and the ball's flight as either a plus (+) or a minus (-). And by that, I don't mean good or bad, and I'm not talking about the symbols for addition and subtraction. A (+) or a (-) simply means how an element of your swing, the ground on which your ball was resting, or the ball's flight relates to the so-called "moment of truth"—impact. **If something is a (+), all I mean is that it's related to influencing an impact to make it steeper and narrower. And if something is a (-), that means it's related to influencing an impact to make it wider and shallower.** Never in the history of golf instruction have these elements been categorized and tied together so simply. All golf swings, even the great ones, contain a varied number of pluses and minuses. But no matter how many pluses and how many minuses you have in your swing, the goal is to have an equal number on each side of the ledger so they balance each other out. Only then can you hit the ball solidly with a repeatable and reliable ball flight.

Since this is a relatively new concept, let me see if I can help you understand it better by comparing it to a topic most of you are familiar with—the U.S. government. The U.S. Senate has one hundred members. Let's say, to a degree, that each of the one hundred senators leans to either the conservative or liberal side of being truly moderate in opinion. And no matter what, they always vote on that side. For decisions to be made without a bias toward conservatism or liberalism, there would then have to be exactly fifty conservative senators and fifty liberal senators. If there wasn't a 50–50 split, the side with a majority would use its influence to make laws that were either conservative or liberal in spirit. Luckily, governments can still function and pass laws despite an unbalanced roster of political views. But a good golf swing can't be achieved without that 50–50 split.

That's why you have to maintain an equal number of pluses and minuses in your swing. Remember when I said earlier that you can improve on your very next shot? Well, here's the beauty of the system presented in this book. By paying attention to your ball flight and, as a secondary confirmation, what the ground looks like where your ball used to be resting (I call that "impact condition"), you can quickly determine whether something you're doing is resulting in a swing that has an odd number of pluses and minuses. If your swing isn't in balance, you will produce poor impact and a ball-flight miss that is a (+) or a (-). It's going to have either one too many elements that results in a steep/narrow impact or one too many that results in a shallow/wide impact. I'm going to teach you how to recognize the error. Then all you'll need to do is refer to the appropriate charts in this book to find out what your swing requires to balance things out. I call that "neutralizing impact." You'll be able to choose from corrections in four different areas of your golf swing: (1) your address position, (2) the backswing, (3) the downswing, (4) impact and the follow-through.

Let me explain my plus/minus system a bit more. As I mentioned above, all golf swings are a combination of pluses and minuses as it relates to impact. But the number of pluses and minuses you have in your swing often depends on your skill level. If you're a scratch golfer and have been playing the game for a while, you probably know that two of the best swings in golf belong to veteran pros Steve Elkington and Ernie Els. Those two guys have refined their swings so well that they probably have very few plus-and-minus swing characteristics. And the fewer pluses and minuses they have, the less they have to balance in order to hit the ball solidly and repetitively. Furthermore, the pluses and minuses in their swings might be minor issues compared to the characteristics in the average 20-handicapper's swing. For Steve and Ernie, their goal might be akin to juggling three plus and three minus tennis balls without dropping one. As long as they keep an even number juggling in the air, their swing is in balance. Each plus ball counters a minus ball. With some practice, the task is fairly easy and routine.

But the typical 20-handicapper has to juggle way more than a few things to achieve solid impact and a consistent ball flight. In some cases, it could be more than ten pluses and ten minuses. What makes the task even harder is that many of those swing elements might be major pluses and minuses. Forget tennis balls. It's like trying to juggle watermelons. It's no wonder high-handicappers struggle to produce John Jacobs's "correct, repetitive impact." They can do it every now and then, probably just enough to not give up and quit golf for good. But their games would be a lot better if they could make their juggling act as simple and routine as Ernie's and Steve's.

I bring this up because there might be times when you'll need to incorporate more than one plus or minus adjustment to your swing in order to balance things out and neutralize impact. In other words, one adjustment isn't going to completely fix a major swing flaw. You might need to implement two or three things to get the job done. Think of the task in terms of cooking. Sometimes a dash of salt isn't enough to get the stew to taste good. So you keep adding salt until you get the right flavor.

So how will you know if you've got a major plus or minus in your swing that needs more TLC than just a minor adjustment to correct? It's simple: If the old ball-flight and impact problems persist even after you make a correction, either exaggerate whatever element you've incorporated or introduce more elements to the mix until your ball flight improves. You'll get immediate feedback that will tell you if what you're doing is enough to fix the problem. If your ball-flight miss is getting worse after you've incorporated something, then you probably misdiagnosed yourself and introduced an element from the wrong category—perhaps you needed a (+) element but you adopted a (-). Don't worry. It's only a short setback. You just need to back up and try an element from the opposite chart. That's the beauty of this book. It doesn't take long to find the right correction and improve. In a later chapter, I'll walk you through the entire process, so don't worry about memorizing it now. I just wanted to give you a taste of what you're going to learn.

To recap what I'm introducing with this book: I've developed a new system that designates everything in your golf swing, along with impact condition and ball flight, as either a plus (narrow/steep) or a minus (wide/shallow). Think of it as your golf DNA. You're going to be able to look at your ball-flight and impact condition and determine whether your swing is either too plus or too minus. You should know that your impact condition and your ball flight will always go together. A (+) impact condition will confirm a (+) ball flight and a (-) impact condition will confirm a (-) ball flight. That's why I'm asking you to pay attention to both your shot shape and the ground on which your ball was resting at address. You will then refer to charts within to look for many options on how to get things back to neutral. Once you even things out, you're going to be able to hit the ball more solidly and with a consistent ball flight. It's as simple as that.

One final thought before we move on to the next chapter: I want you to understand that a golf shot is the result of three actions—the swing, the swing's resulting impact, and the impact's resulting ball flight. Ball flight, and to a lesser degree, the ground where your ball used to be, tell you what's wrong with your swing. You're like a detective at a crime scene trying to piece together the clues. To help you, I've committed chapters to all of the ball-flight misses and explain why each one is either a (+) or a (-) and what to do about it. You'd be surprised at how many golfers are obsessed with different facets of their swing but are still never able to figure out what's wrong. What they should be paying attention to is what happens when the club meets the ball. That information, if they know how to use it, will not only tell them what's wrong but will lead them to a solution that will allow them to fix it. Once you're able to successfully recognize the (+) or (-) value of your ball flight and the ground beneath the ball at impact, you can then link those two elements back to the (+) or (-) swing issues that caused them. That's how you can be your own golf instructor, and that's how you can improve your ball-striking on the very next shot.

SOLID
CONTACT

Chapter One

THE KEY ELEMENTS OF IMPACT

As I stated in the introduction, the purpose of this book is to present my revolutionary plus/minus system and show you how to use it, so you can diagnose your own swing flaws and then learn how to correct them. The goal is for you to hit the ball more solidly than ever and with a consistent ball flight. Notice that I didn't say the goal is to get you to hit the ball straight. That's because you don't have to play a straight ball to play good golf. Just look at all those pros I mentioned previously. Guys such as Nicklaus, Watson, Trevino, and Player all relied on different ball flights to win countless tournaments. That's not to say I don't want to see you improve your current ball flight. And that's not to say that I don't like a straight ball. Heck, who doesn't like a straight ball? But it's far more important to learn how to hit solid shots and to be confident that you know where the ball is going than it is to spend years on the range trying to copy the swing of a computer model in order to hit it perfectly straight.

Now, let's discuss the importance of recognizing your typical ball flight and why the ball flies the way it does. John Jacobs was the first instructor to really teach students by analyzing their ball flights. "Look at what the ball is doing and then ask why," he'd say. John is a genius and always knew the answer to "Why?"—and with the help of this book, you're going to know the answer, too. If you want to fix your problems, I can't stress enough that you're going to have to pay attention to your ball flight. I'm sure there are times when you'll want to look away in disgust—especially when that shot is curving toward a water hazard or a house. But seriously, what the ball's doing will tell you what you need to do to improve, so I'm asking you to pay careful attention.

With that said, I think it's time to give you a better understanding of what determines the direction, curvature, and trajectory of a golf shot. There are several impact factors, such as the club's shape, the speed it was traveling at impact, the launch angle and spin rate of the ball, etc. All of those things come into play, but they're not nearly as significant as the four variables I'd like you to focus on: **(1) the position of the clubface, (2) clubpath, (3) the angle of approach, and (4) the width of the bottom of the swing.**

The first element of impact I'd like to discuss is **the position of the clubface when it meets the ball.** Years ago, before the advent of perimeter-weighted clubs and high-tech ball designs, the clubface's primary influence on the ball was how it made the ball curve (or not curve) after impact. For instance, if the clubface was closed to the direction the club was moving at impact, then the ball hooked to the left (for right-handed swingers). Conversely, if the clubface was open to the path the club was traveling at impact, then the ball sliced to the right. If you happened to get the clubface square to the path at impact, then the ball wouldn't curve at all—it would fly straight. It might fly straight right or straight left depending on the path the club was swinging on at impact, but the ball would fly on a line. It's simple physics. With today's technological improvements in golf equipment, less sidespin is being imparted on the ball, so the curvature of the ball's flight isn't as pronounced and is much harder to identify. Nowadays, a closed or open clubface at impact is more likely to influence the direction the ball will travel rather than just the curvature of the ball's flight. By that I mean that if the face were, say, pointing left of your target at impact, the ball would also go left of your target. An open clubface will result in the ball flying right of your target. The sidespin caused by an open or closed face isn't what it used to be, so shots typically have less hook or slice curvature. A secondary influence that the clubface has on impact is to make it either steeper (+) or shallower (-). I will explain the (+) and (-) system in detail in a moment, but for now, **remember that a clubface that is closed (pointing left for right-handed swingers) to the path will make an impact steeper, while an open clubface to the path will make impact shallower.** In other words, when you close the clubface, it becomes a digging tool, with the leading edge and toe carving a significant divot out of the ground. An open clubface, however, rides along the ground on the back of the club (commonly known as the "bounce") and creates a shallow divot, if any.

Now that you have a better understanding of how the position of the clubface at impact influences ball flight, let's move on to the second direct cause of impact: **clubpath.** The club's path at impact and how it influences ball flight is more complicated than the clubface's role. If you were to look at the clubpath from a camera directly above a right-handed golfer, you'd see that during the downswing and follow-through, the clubhead travels on an arc that moves from behind the body to the right side of the body to the area in front of the body, then over to the left side, and finally back around the body again. In a technically correct golf swing viewed from overhead, the arc the clubhead travels on during the downswing will go from inside the target line, then along the target line, and then back inside the target line. The distance the clubhead actually travels along the target line is very small—less than an inch or two—and, measured in time, just a few ten-thousandths of a second. Therefore, a technically perfect path is described as an arc that is **in-to-in** (inside the target line, then on the line, then back inside the target line). If your path isn't perfect, then it's either in-to-out or out-to-in. **In-to-out** paths mean that the clubhead is moving to the right of the target at impact (for right-handed golfers) and **out-to-in** arcs mean the club is moving to the left at impact. These three different paths will produce different impact conditions by influencing both the angle of approach and, inevitably, the direction the ball flies.

First, let me explain how clubpath influences the angle of approach. If a swing path arc is in-to-out, it makes the angle of approach shallow (-). This is because an in-to-out path bottoms out and reaches its low point before the clubhead contacts the ball. It's actually ascending when it makes contact. Conversely, if the path is out-to-in, it makes the approach steep (+). An out-to-in path is the opposite of an in-to-out path—the swing doesn't bottom out and reach the low point until it's just in front of the ball. What that means is that the clubhead is still swinging down too steeply on its arc when it contacts the ball. Now comes the second part. The influence that clubpath has on the flight of the ball is determined when the direction is compared to the position of the clubface at impact. If the clubface is square to the path at impact, the ball will fly in the direction of the path. If the path was, say, out-to-in, and the clubface was square to the path, then the ball would fly on a straight line, left of the target. This is known as a "pull." Conversely, an in-to-out path with a square clubface to the path will produce a straight right shot known as a "push." With today's equipment, the more the clubface is open or closed in relation to the path, the more the ball will go in the direction of the face.

To further understand how the clubface and path work together, let's take two different ball flights that fly right of your intended target. One would be a slice, in which the clubface is open to the path, and the other is a push, in which the clubface is square to an in-to-out path. The slice is a glancing blow and not powerful, while the push is fairly powerful. Although the ball ends up right of your target with either a slice or a push, the ball flights look somewhat different from each other. But for argument's sake, let's just say you can't tell them apart. If you want to know which is which, just take a look at the ground where impact occurred. If you happened to take a divot, study the clubhead's mark or hole in the ground. That mark in the ground is the divot's telltale evidence. (When I use the term "divot," I'm referring to the mark or hole in the ground on or near the spot on which your ball was resting at address. I don't mean the strip of sod that you hopefully pick up and replace to help tidy the golf course.) So if the ball flew right of the divot's direction, you hit a slice. The only way the ball got to the right of the swing path (direction of the divot) was because the clubface was open to the path. If the ball moved in the same direction as the divot, then you pushed the shot. This works the same if the ball was hit to the left. If the ball traveled left of the divot mark, then it went left because of a closed clubface and would be considered a hook (I also refer to this in the book as a "slap-left")—even though it might not have curved very much. But if the ball went left and the divot is pointing in the same direction to the left, you've hit a pull. I mentioned in the introduction that impact condition is a secondary yet important clue in determining your ball flight. In later chapters, I'll go over this in more detail.

So to summarize to this point, you should know that the club's path at impact is a determinant of the angle of approach. If the path is in-to-out, the angle will be shallow (-). If the path is out-to-in, the angle will be steep (+). The path will also affect the direction of the ball. When the clubface is square to the path, you will push your shot if your path is in-to-out and pull it if it's out-to-in. Otherwise, if the clubface is not square to the path, the direction of the ball is predominately determined by where the clubface was pointing when it struck the ball.

Now let's move on to the third primary influencer of impact—**the angle of approach**. The angle primarily determines the trajectory of the shot (high, medium, or low), but it also influences the amount of backspin on the ball. Simply put, the angle of approach is the amount the clubhead is swinging up, down, or level to the ground when it strikes the ball. Every shot and every club requires a specific angle of approach—if the club isn't swung down to the ball on this angle, it's very difficult to hit a solid shot with a repeatable ball flight. A tee shot with a driver, for example, requires a shallow (level or upward) angle of approach, but a short-iron shot off a downhill lie requires a steep downward angle of approach.

The good news is that you can hit all your clubs correctly without having to adjust the angle on every shot. I'll explain why later. But for now, it's important to simply understand that the more the clubhead strikes the ball on a downward angle, the more the ball will slide up the clubface and fly on a higher trajectory. In addition, the steeper the angle of attack, the more backspin will be imparted to the ball. Conversely, on shots hit off the ground, the shallower the angle of approach at impact, the less the ball will roll up the clubface. It will fly lower and spin less.

I've saved the fourth major element of impact—**the width of the bottom of the swing**—for last, because it's rarely, if ever, been discussed. In fact, to my knowledge, this book is the first time it has ever been defined in great detail. What do I mean by the width of the bottom of the swing? Imagine viewing someone's golf swing from a face-on position, as though you turned around to watch the guy behind you at the driving range hit a shot. From this perspective, you can see that the swing has different segments relative to the ground. At address, the club is resting on the ground. It's at the bottom of its swing arc. But as the golfer makes a backswing, the clubhead first moves fairly close to the ground and then gradually ascends until the golfer reaches the top of the swing. This path is then reversed and the club heads toward the ground. Through impact, it rides along the ground and then ascends again as the golfer completes his swing. Now think of that swing motion as having a bottom, a top and two sides. The width of the bottom of the swing is the part when the clubhead is moving through the impact zone and fairly tangent to the ground. By looking at the swing from the face-on perspective, and by paying attention to how long the clubhead is tangent to the ground, you can tell if the bottom is wide or narrow.

Here's another way of understanding this element. Think for a moment about how airplanes land at the airport. Those monster 747 passenger airliners have to approach the runway on a very shallow angle, and they need a lot of pavement in order to come to a safe stop. But small, single-engine planes, especially aerobatic planes, can make an approach on a much steeper angle and require far less runway to stop. The amount of runway required for the airplane is analogous to the width of the bottom of the swing. Each type of airplane requires a different landing pattern and a different amount of runway. The same holds true for your golf clubs.

The Scots were pretty clever when they invented this game. They figured out that the loft of each club also determines the necessary length of the clubshaft. The less loft on a club, the more the clubhead was intended to meet the ball near the ball's equator. But the clubheads that were designed with more loft were intended to strike the ball closer to its bottom. Some smart clubmakers figured out that if they used a longer shaft for the less-lofted clubs, it accomplished a couple of things that helped to strike the ball near its equator. The longer shaft put the ball farther from the golfer, and it set the shaft on an angle at both address and impact that was more level with the ground. Both of these factors naturally force the golfer to swing these clubs on a shallower angle of approach with a wider bottom to the swing. Stated differently, the driver's design is trying to make it easier for you to swing the clubhead along the ground and into the equator of the ball.

Meanwhile, those same clubmakers figured out that the clubs with more loft needed shorter shafts. A shorter shaft means you have to stand closer to the ball, which in turn promotes a more upright shaft angle at address and impact.

The shorter shaft also reduces the length the clubhead is fairly tangent to the ground through impact, creating a narrower width to the bottom of the swing. That's the long way of saying it made it a lot easier for golfers to swing down, under, and back up again through the ball.

How smart were those Scots? Well, those early design principles are still used today. Every club requires a different width to the bottom of the swing in order to be used optimally. For instance, a driver with a 45-inch shaft needs to make a shallower angle of approach and have a wider swing bottom through the ball in order to do its job correctly. It needs to skirt along the ground for the longest distance of any club in the bag. It's a lot like that 747 jumbo jet. But a sand wedge can come down into the ball on a much steeper angle of approach with a narrower bottom, which allows you to swing the clubhead down, under, and back up again through the ball. The width of the bottom of the swing for a wedge is short, especially compared to the driver, fairway woods, and longer irons. It's like that aerobatic plane.

That's why the width of the bottom of the swing—your runway—is very important to your ability to reach your goal of solid shots with a repetitive ball flight. It helps control the consistency, height, and solidness of the hit. How many times have you found yourself hitting your irons really well but struggling with your driver, or vice versa? You'll often hear tour pros say they were really pounding the driver during a round but not having as much luck with their irons. There are also pros who are known for their excellent iron play or their prowess off the tee, but rarely do you hear a pro complimented for both. Remember, each club has an ideal length for its runway, and if the bottom of the swing is too wide/long or too narrow/short, you're going to struggle to hit solid shots with all of your clubs.

Now, as I mentioned earlier, I'm not saying you should adjust the bottom of your swing every time you pull a different club from the bag. I realize it would be too hard even for professionals to adjust the width of the bottom of the swing from shot to shot. So instead, the goal is to consistently make swings where the width is neither too narrow nor too wide for any club. If your swing width is fairly neutral, you'll be able to play all your clubs effectively. If you think about the airport analogy one more time, what you ideally want is a medium-length runway that is appropriate for all types of planes. The reason this works is because the different shaft lengths of each club will help lengthen, or reduce, that medium-length runway to its ideal length for that particular club by making you stand closer or farther away from the ball. That's the beauty of club design. If your swing bottom is neutral, then the club's shaft length will make your swing bottom either shallow/wide or steep/narrow, depending on what you need to hit that shot solidly. Problems occur when the width of the bottom of your swing is either too narrow or too wide. If it's too narrow, then you'll struggle with the longer clubs. And if it's too wide, the shorter clubs will be difficult for you.

Now that you have a better understanding of the four major elements of impact (the position of the clubface at impact, the club's path through the ball, the angle of approach into the ball, and the width of the bottom of the swing), take a guess at which of those are the most important in terms of hitting solid shots and having a consistent ball flight. Hopefully my runway analogy was the giveaway clue. The answer is the angle of approach and width of the bottom of the swing.

These two elements are the keys to this book. They are the basis of your swing's DNA. Every ball-flight miss I will discuss in later chapters is the result of having the incorrect angle of approach (otherwise known as angle of attack) and/or width of the bottom of the swing. An important point about these two elements: Angle of approach is primarily responsible for hitting the ball flush—one of your two goals—while the width of the bottom of the swing is mostly responsible for producing a predictable/repetitive ball flight (the other goal).

These two impact elements usually go together, but it should be noted that they don't always. For instance, you can have a swing with a narrow (+) width at the bottom. But if your club's path is severely in-to-out, you could be swinging up and into the ball on a shallow angle of approach (-). Another example: You could have an overly wide bottom of the swing (-) if you stand too far away from the ball and swing your arms and club very flat. But if your path is too much out-to-in, your angle of approach will be steep (+). In other words, don't automatically assume that if your angle of approach is steep (+), the width of the bottom of the swing is narrow (+). These two elements of impact definitely are independent of each other. However, after decades of studying golf swings, I've come to the conclusion that the net effect the two have on impact is the same. I'll repeat that. You should pair the terms of shallow/wide (-) and steep/narrow (+) together with regard to the effect they have upon impact, even though they describe different parts of impact. I'd also add that it's very rare that a (+) or (-) angle of approach isn't matched up with the same (+) or (-) width of the bottom of the swing. I'd say in almost every case, if the swing is creating a steep angle of approach, it has the same effect as having too narrow a swing bottom. And if the approach is shallow, it has the same effect of a wide swing bottom. Therefore, consider them interchangeable.

Now that you have a better understanding of the elements of impact, you're ready for an in-depth explanation of my plus/minus system and how you can use it to neutralize your golf swing and hit solid and repetitive shots.

Chapter Two

NARROW/STEEP VS. WIDE/SHALLOW

Y ou might be wondering how I came up with this plus/minus concept. Well, I travel a lot and spend a great deal of time at the airport, and it got me thinking about how planes land. As I explained in the previous chapter, I realized it was the perfect analogy for how the club moves through the impact zone. In the case of the (+) symbol, the vertical line reminded me of an airplane that's approaching the runway on far too steep an angle and would certainly have too short a runway to land safely. The (-) symbol made me think about an airplane that just keeps circling the airport in a holding pattern. Its angle of approach is so shallow that the passengers are all wondering if they're ever going to land. And even if the plane did touch down, its approach is so shallow that it would need an extremely long runway to avoid crashing into neighborhood homes, power lines, trees, etc., usually short of the runway.

I knew I could build on this concept and apply it to the golf swing once I discovered that all swing elements influence impact by making it more of a (+) or (-). If I could get golfers to understand that everything in their golf swing, the impact condition, and their ball flight could either be designated as a (+) or a (-), then I could get them to fix their own swings by understanding that the elements on the opposite side would neutralize whatever problem they were having. It was an exciting prospect, to say the least, since most golf instruction prior to this book was focused on the swing and not on ball flight as the primary method for correcting mistakes.

Your ball flight might be a push or a pull, or a hook or a fade, but if you use the plus/minus system, you'll be able to count on hitting that push, pull, hook, or fade solidly, while simply adjusting your aim accordingly so that the ball lands where you want it to. Whether you swing on one plane or two, whether you swing like Nicklaus or Trevino, you'll be able to enjoy the game more because you can hit solid shots with a predictable ball flight. Even if you're a golfer who wants to build a swing around a particular model, the plus/minus system will tell you when you have either exaggerated or underdone a particular swing movement. For instance, if you're a one-plane advocate, the system will tell you when you need to get your arms flatter or your weight more on your left leg or your shoulder turn steeper. It will tell you exactly which swing element within your pattern you need to pay attention to.

By now, you hopefully understand how a balance of pluses and minuses in your swing will produce solid contact and a reliable ball flight. A balanced swing is what I call a neutral swing. Same with a good shot that is solid and predictable—I call it a neutral shot. A neutral swing produces a neutral impact, which in turn produces a neutral shot pattern. But what we haven't discussed to this point is what happens when your swing isn't in balance and is either too (+) or too (-). Unfortunately, an unbalanced swing will cause an unbalanced impact, and you'll mishit the ball. It's a chain reaction. All ball-flight misses are the result of a swing that has more pluses than minuses, or vice versa. To better understand this chain, let's get back to the fundamentals of the system. If all swings are mixtures of things that influence impact to be either narrow and steep (+) or wide and shallow (-), then everything you do in your swing, from how you stand at address right on through to your clubpath at impact, will play a role in what the ball does. Some things have a greater influence on impact than others, but they all influence it in some way.

To give you some examples of what I mean when I say that everything influences impact, let's say that I'm fairly bent over at address. This, in turn, makes me move my shoulders on a steeper plane, which influences impact by making it more steep/narrow (+). But if I stood taller, my shoulders would move more level with the ground as I swung the club, and that would influence an impact that's more toward the shallow/wide (-) end of things. Now let's say I keep my weight more on my left foot as I take the club back. That's another (+) element. If my weight is more on my right foot, that's a (-) element. An upright arm swing? You guessed it. It's a (+). But a flat arm swing is a (-). If the clubshaft is pointing to the right of my target at the top of my backswing (known as being "across the line"), that position is a (+). If the shaft is pointing left of my target at the top of my backswing (known as being "laid off"), that position is a (-). Other examples: head moving to the left (+), head moving to the right (-); early wrist set (+), late wrist set (-); slide my hips laterally in the downswing (-), turn my hips to the left in the downswing (+). I could keep going and going, but I think you get the point: There are potentially a lot of things in your swing that can make it either too (+) or too (-). A golf swing is actually built on these opposite factors. For instance, for one-planers, the more they bend over and turn their shoulders fairly steeply (+), the more they need to swing their arms and club somewhat flatter around their bodies (-). Conversely, for two-planers, the straighter they stand and turn their shoulders flat (-), the more they naturally need to swing their arms and club upright (+). It's when we lose these offsetting elements in our swings that we get out-of-balance impacts and, inevitably, out-of-balance ball flights.

And as I said earlier, there are many elements that are very minor in terms of how they affect impact. For example, flaring your right foot out at address allows you to make a bigger backswing turn, which is a (-) characteristic. And if you turned your left foot out at address, it restricts your backswing turn, which is a (+) characteristic. But neither foot adjustment is going to do a lot to affect impact. I bring this up because for the sake of our goals with this book, I don't want you to be too concerned with the minor influencing elements. For the most part, these little adjustments, like flaring a foot, are just signatures that make our swings unique.

What you should be concerned with are the elements of your swing that have a major influence on the (+) or (-) result at impact. How do you know which are major and which are minor? I'm going to provide charts (pages 45–46) that will list only the major swing elements and identify whether they fall into the (+) or (-) category. There will be charts listing all of the major plus and minus elements of address, the backswing, the downswing, and impact/follow-through. The key to understanding how these elements affect impact is to view them in their dynamic state. By that I mean the degree to which an element is present in your swing. For instance, the influence on impact of bending over more at address (+) depends on how much you bend over. If your address posture is fairly neutral—not too upright and not too hunched over—then this element is minor and it won't have a significant impact on your ball flight. But if you start bending over more or standing taller, then suddenly this element will have a major influence on impact and the subsequent ball flight. Another way of looking at this would be if you tended to stand very tall at address. If you made an adjustment and started to bend over more, the more you did it, the more you would be making your swing, impact, and ball flight steeper/narrower (+).

Therefore, each of the swing elements listed in the charts should be considered in an adjustable sense. The more you move that element in one direction or the other, the more it becomes a major influence on impact, making it either (+) or (-). I want you to understand this because it goes a long way toward explaining why tour pros hit the ball more solidly and repetitively than amateurs. A tour pro might be juggling a half dozen swing elements that are pluses and a half dozen that are minuses. But as I pointed out with Ernie Els's and Steve Elkington's swings, none of the elements are too pronounced. So it's no wonder that those guys can balance the ledger almost every time they hit a shot. Every now and then, they might let one of the pluses or minuses in their swing become more exaggerated, which throws their balance of pluses and minuses out of whack. That's when you see them hit a bad shot. But it doesn't happen often, and that's why tour pros make millions playing the game. The typical amateur golfer, however, has far more pluses and minuses to deal with. Even worse, some of these swing elements are so exaggerated that it takes a Herculean effort to get them to balance. When balance does occur, this golfer hits a good shot. But the number and severity of the pluses and minuses makes juggling them consistently nearly impossible. Remember my analogy about juggling tennis balls versus juggling watermelons?

Pretend for a minute that you're a high-handicapper who reverse-pivots by shifting nearly all of your weight onto your front foot during the backswing. Or maybe you don't have to pretend . . . kidding. But let's say you shift your weight that way and also take the club back with a very steep shoulder turn. Both of these moves are common mistakes for high-handicappers and are major pluses. Now, in order to hit the ball, you have to counter the reverse pivot and steep shoulder turn by incorporating some major minuses into your swing. The pluses and minuses have to balance. One way you can counter the reverse pivot is by shifting your weight onto your back foot (-) as you swing down. You then counter the steep shoulder turn by swinging up on the ball through impact (-). Every time you accomplish this feat, you hit a pretty good shot for your skill level. It might not be a powerful draw, but the fade it produces is far better than the chop slice you would have hit if you didn't get the pluses and minuses to balance out.

What separates this book from traditional golf instruction is what would happen if you went and got a lesson instead of following the advice here. Too often, the pro will take a five-minute look at this fall-back-on-the-right-foot downswing issue and tell you to shift more weight onto your front foot and swing more down into the ball. It's advice that's given time and time again, and with good intentions. But in your case, what this advice does is make your swing worse. If you were to try to become more orthodox in your downswing and shift more weight onto your left foot and move forward into impact, you would suddenly start slamming your club into the ground. If you didn't break your wrists, or club, you could probably make a divot deep enough to plant a tree. Why would this happen? Think about it. You already had two major (+) elements in your swing. When you check the charts in this book, you'll see that moving more weight into the left foot during the downswing also is a (+) element. You were told to do this because it's a fundamental of a prototype golf swing. You want your weight shifting into your front foot as you swing down. But you didn't have a prototype golf swing. So by shifting weight into your front foot, you just added another (+) to your juggling act. What you really needed was two minuses to balance out your swing elements. You would have been much better off saving your money on the golf lessons and using this book.

In order to improve, you should have paid attention to your ball flight and impact conditions. As I mentioned, you predominantly hit chop slices, which is a (+). You also took deep divots, which confirmed that your ball flight was a (+). So you can deduce that your swing is narrow/steep. You would then go to the charts and try as many minus swing elements as necessary to start hitting the ball solidly and with a predictable ball flight.

Remember, the more the swing is out of balance, the more severe the (+) or (-) impact becomes and the more severe the ball-flight miss will be. If you think of your ball-flight miss in terms of a (+) or a (-), you'll begin to understand your impact issues and finally get a handle on why your swing isn't neutral. That's why I call the plus/minus system your swing's DNA code. To unlock that code and figure out how to improve, you have to start from the result (ball flight) and then move back to impact and finally back to your swing. Most golf instruction starts by looking at the swing, but that's a mistake and a big reason why so many golfers don't improve and quit the game. If you start by paying attention to your ball flight and are able to read it correctly, you won't make a mistake when you're trying to understand what to do to improve your swing.

Your ball-flight miss will be in a category that is either a (+) or a (-) as it relates to impact. Descriptions of the various misses will be discussed in later chapters, so I'll help you make sure you read your ball-flight miss correctly. But just as in the example of you as a high-handicapper who reverse-pivoted and took a lot of deep divots, a way to verify that you've read your ball-flight miss correctly is to look at the ground where your ball used to be resting (impact condition). If the ball-flight miss was a (+), then the impact condition also has to also be a (+). And vice versa for minuses. In the chapters on the various ball-flight misses, I will list the impact evidence you'll be looking for to help verify your issue. There might be times when you can't find any corroborating evidence. For instance, you might be slicing, which is a (+) ball-flight miss, but you shift your weight so far onto your back foot during the downswing that you don't take any divot. So how will you accurately identify your ball-flight miss? In the chapter that discusses slicing, it will tell you that you should see a deep divot pointing to the left of your target. It might not be present if you only take a couple of swings, but if you hit enough balls, sooner or later you'll see that ground condition.

Now let's move on. Assuming that you've correctly identified your ball-flight miss and confirmed it with your typical impact condition, it's time to apply the plus/minus system to your swing. As I mentioned earlier, to complete this task I've supplied charts identifying the major elements of address, the backswing, the downswing, and impact/follow-through. If your ball-flight miss and impact condition confirm that you're too (+) or too (-), you simply take one element from the other side of the chart and incorporate it into your swing. There are literally dozens of adjustments you can make to even things out. So many, in fact, that you're probably wondering how you decide what to choose and how much of that element you'll need to apply. That's the beauty of this system. It doesn't really matter what you pick as long as you're fixing a (+) swing mistake by neutralizing it with a (-) fix or a (-) swing mistake with a (+) fix. And you'll know exactly how much of that element you'll need to apply simply by comparing your old shots to your new (and hopefully improved) ones.

Having said that, there are some elements that fix a ball-flight miss more easily and quicker than others. So if left to your own devices, it might take some trial and error before you find something that "clicks" with you. That's why, to save you time, I've included in the chapters on the various ball-flight misses some recommendations on which elements seem to work the best for that particular problem. I've culled these fixes from years of working with students of all abilities. But I want to reiterate that regardless of the element you use, when you start the process, the element has to be from the opposite category of your ball-flight miss. If your dressing is too oily, you don't add more oil. You add vinegar. And you keep adding until it tastes just right. Same principle here.

Your ball, and hopefully the smile on your face, will tell you when you've added the right amount of the opposite element. Some of you might have to add a LOT of vinegar to get that taste just right, while others might only need a dash. You'll know you've got your swing back to neutral when your shots become more solid, with a consistent ball flight. If you were a slicer, your shots might still tail off to the right after incorporating an opposite element to your swing. But that fade you're now hitting will be hit a lot more solidly. Same thing if you were hooking shots. With the right adjustment, that hook will look a lot more like a draw. Better still, you'll be able to repeat that ball flight enough to keep your ball in play and lower your scores.

This brings me back to the golf greats—Nicklaus, Trevino, Player, and Watson. They didn't worry about hitting the ball dead straight. They worried about getting the ball from Point A to Point B. They all hit solid shots with a reliable ball flight. I know that hubris comes into play, and that we all want a pretty swing, but I'm asking you to forget that notion and work with your swing's own DNA. Whether your shot pattern is high or low or a fade or a draw, or your method is one-plane or two-plane, as long as your shots are solid and the flight is repetitive, you're on your way to better golf.

Now that you understand how my plus/minus system works, it's time to show you how to apply it. Most, but not all, of you can simply incorporate one element to your current swing and you'll start hitting shots more solidly with a repetitive ball flight. The rest of you, however, are going to have to use the system to incorporate two fixes to your swing in order to start seeing better results. Both paths are easily navigated, and in the next chapter, I'm going to tell you which path you need to take and why.

Chapter Three

HOW TO APPLY THE SYSTEM

I n all my years of teaching, I've found that there are two types of golfers who come to me for a lesson: golfers who need to fix only one thing in their swings to improve, and golfers who need to fix two things to improve. Those are the only two golfers I teach, and in my opinion, the only two types of golfers that exist. I'm not a believer that you have to totally change your swing to play better. I'm sure a lot of people would recommend that Jim Furyk, Bubba Watson, and Rickie Fowler change the unique way they swing the club. But it's hard to argue with their success. How about Matt Kuchar? In 2010, Kuchar was the leading money winner, had the lowest scoring average, and was the all-around statistical leader on the PGA Tour. Yet it seemed like every time you turned on the television, people were criticizing his swing because they thought it wasn't pretty enough. Matt laughed all the way to the bank.

With the advent of stop-action/slow-motion video, where

instructors can analyze every millisecond of a golfer's swing, I believe the golf world took many steps backward in terms of teaching. The focus shifted to swing models and trying to force swings into molds that are pleasing to the eye. But what has been lost is the ability to fix whatever swing—pretty or ugly, textbook or unusual—a golfer has developed and make it work. It seems that whenever golfers start hitting a few bad shots, they are told they will have to totally rebuild their swings. The truly sad part of this trend is that golfers have bought into it, including some of the greatest players in the world. It's as though no one knows how to fix or refine a swing, and the only alternative is to rebuild it and hope that, after months or years of implementation, it will work better than the original swing.

I attribute this terrible trend to a fixation on swing shape and a total disregard for impact and ball flight. From reading the previous chapters, you already know how strongly I feel about ball flight and impact and that the sole purpose of a golf swing is to produce solid contact and a reliable shot shape. The method employed is not significant as long as it is repetitive. Now, a lot of golfers want to change their swings because there are certain shots or clubs they struggle to hit effectively. But I believe this is a fool's errand. I assure you, Lee Trevino struggled mightily to hit a high powerful draw, so he rarely tried. Tom Watson didn't hit a lot of low shots, and Arnold Palmer almost never went with a fade. Golfers who want to change their swings often get worse, because they try to learn a swing that doesn't fit their style, athletic ability, or learning process. Instead of trying to master the swing they have, their obsession with adopting another swing leads to frustration and failure. My question is, why change? I didn't see Jack Nicklaus overhaul his swing each time he fell into a slump. I haven't seen Furyk try to get rid of his trade-mark loop, and I watched Billy Casper win 51 PGA Tour events by mostly playing an ugly, low-running shot. I wonder how any of them would have done if they had bagged what they already had and started over? Even Ben Hogan, whom many consider the greatest swinger of all time, stuck with his style, even when he was failing. He just kept refining it, kept fixing it.

The students I teach are no different, and as I mentioned earlier, I see them as falling into two categories—they're either one-plane or two-plane swingers. I just keep fixing and refining their swings based on their own style of play. My goal and theirs is to produce solid shots and predictable ball flight. Their ball flights and impacts tell me what to do to help them achieve our goals, just as, with the aid of this book, your impacts and ball flights will hopefully tell you what to do to improve your game.

Now let's look at the two types of golfers. I call them either a "**one-fix**" or a "**two-fix**" golfer. A golfer who might fall into the one-fix category is a tour pro who has missed the last five cuts because his or her normal draw has turned into a full-blown hook. It could also be an 18-handicapper who is now playing like a 25 because he or she suddenly can't get the ball off the ground. If you were consistent within your level of ability for a decent period, but are no longer playing like you used to, then you're probably going to fall into the one-fix category. The reason for this sudden drop-off in performance is that you no longer are balancing the (+) and (-) elements in your swing. You were successful in juggling a manageable number and size of pluses and minuses, but now you're struggling to hit solid shots, because you've either picked up a new (+) or (-) element in your swing, or one of the older pluses or minuses has grown in significance and you now can't juggle them consistently. In other words, you have more pluses or minuses in your swing than normal, or one of your swing elements has grown in significance and knocked your swing out of whack. The place in your swing where the problem originates might be in any of these four segments: address, backswing, downswing, or impact/follow-through.

Just as the name implies, a one-fix golfer needs to incorporate only one (+) or (-) element to improve, and that golfer can choose from dozens of options in the four swing segments to get the job done. In other words, if you're a one-fix golfer, your problem will be easy to solve. Want even more good news? I'd say that about 75 to 85 percent of all golfers are in the one-fix category. The remaining 15 to 25 percent are in the two-fix category and will have a more difficult task correcting their problems. I'll explain what they need to do later in this chapter, but for now, let's get back to the one-fix golfers.

To use this book correctly, all you have to do is identify your ball-flight miss and confirm it by checking your impact conditions. Then diagnose whether you have too many elements in your swing that are shallow/wide (-) or steep/narrow (+). And then incorporate one thing from the opposite side of the plus/minus charts to help get your swing back to neutral. You might have ten elements in your swing that would be pluses in my charts. But that's fine as long as you also have ten minuses. You probably aren't going to play on the PGA Tour if you're juggling all those things—especially if a few of them are major elements—but if you can balance them out, you'll be able to hit the ball solidly enough and predictably enough to score better and enjoy a round of golf. When you're a one-fix golfer, your problem is that you can normally hit good shots with decent or better consistency, but you're simply not doing that right now. You're out of balance—either too (+) or too (-). To neutralize that, introduce an element from the opposite side of the ledger and keep increasing the amount of that element until you're back to neutral and playing solid golf again. And remember, because you have so many options to choose from to fix your swing, you should go with an element that works easily for you.

Now let's talk about two-fix golfers. Golfers who fall into this category are usually having trouble with consistency. And I don't necessarily mean rank beginners. A two-fix golfer might be a tour pro, a low-handicapper, a 25-handicapper, or someone in between. These golfers hit really good shots from time to time, but never know when the next bad shot will show up. A typical round for a two-fix candidate might include a couple of pars, maybe a birdie, but also a couple of double or even triple bogeys. Another two-fix candidate might be a single-digit handicapper who has a great short game but can't get it together off the tee. Some tee shots go straight right. Others wildly left. Some are low and others high, and this golfer has to rely on scrambling to score.

The problem facing two-fix golfers is the size of the elements they are juggling and the fact that they have a significant (+) or (-) element in the first half of their swings and a significant, but opposite, compensation (+) or (-) element in the second half of their swings. Because the first-half element and the compensating second-half element are so large, the swing can quickly get out of balance either way. It can go from in balance to (+), then (-), and then back in balance again. Recalling a metaphor I used in earlier chapters, it's like juggling watermelons. That's the main difference between one-fix golfers and two-fix golfers. As I stated earlier, one-fix golfers have one too many pluses or minuses in their swings. It might be at address, during the backswing, during the downswing, or during the impact/follow-through phase. But the bottom line is that even though the plus/minus elements aren't in balance, the problem isn't that severe. They are juggling tennis balls and can correct their problems quite easily. Two-fix golfers, on the other hand, are juggling those watermelons. Because both the top-of-backswing (+) or (-) element and the compensating downswing or impact/follow-through (+) or (-) elements are so large, trying to balance things out shot after shot is very difficult.

Now you might think that since they have (+) and (-) elements in their swings, two-fix golfers are going to produce both (+) and (-) ball flights equally. If that was the case, they'd have a heck of a time trying to determine their predominant ball-flight miss. But it doesn't work that way. I'd say that about 95 percent of the time, the (+) or (-) nature of the second half of the two-fix golfer's swing will be the one that dictates whether it's a (+) or (-) ball-flight miss. The reason for this is that the compensation move in the second half of the swing overrides whatever mistake happened in the first half. To use another metaphor from an earlier chapter, the compensation move is the one that has to try to land the plane safely. Think of an airplane approaching the runway on too steep of an angle. The pilot will have to try to level the plane off before it crashes. This is the compensation move. If the pilot doesn't do it exactly right, he or she will almost always err on the safe side and pull up too quickly.

Getting back to the golf swing, if you have a severely steep backswing (a watermelon-size plus), you will also swing down too steeply and bury your club into the ground unless you make some kind of effort to shallow things out. That often means abruptly swinging up on the ball (a watermelon-size minus). You're the pilot and you're trying to pull up. But if you don't time it just right, this will probably cause you to top or thin the shot. In short, your abrupt effort to swing up on the ball dictated what happened at impact, and you produced a (-) ball flight.

The same thing works if the top-of-backswing position is too (-). The compensation move in the second half of the swing—a (+)—will almost always override the first-half problem and produce a (+) ball flight. If we go back to our pilot analogy, this time he's flying on such a flat level that he'll never land the plane unless he steepens his angle of approach. The landing might be bumpy and rough, but it was the steepening adjustment that got the plane on the ground. So in summary, although it's not absolute, the overwhelming majority of two-fix golfers will only hit ball-flight misses on one side of the chart or the other.

So what do two-fix golfers need to do to start hitting solid shots with a repeatable ball flight? They will first have to incorporate a (+) or (-) swing element to discover if they are, in fact, a one- or a two-fix golfer. They won't know until the first new element is introduced into their swing. If they neutralize the swing after incorporating this first element, then they were actually a one-fix golfer. However, if after they've applied one element, they have a new ball flight and it's on the other side of the plus/minus charts from their original problem, then they will know they are truly in the two-fix category.

To give you an example, let's say you normally hit shots from a (-) ball-flight category such as pushes, hooks, fats, or thins. You then incorporate a (+) element, but instead of acquiring a solid, repeatable ball flight, you now have developed a (+) ball-flight miss such as a pull, slice, chop, or chunk.

If that happens, you're a two-fix golfer because your miss just went to the opposite category, from a (-) to a (+). In other words, your results when you correctly apply the system will tell you whether you need only one fix or if you need two.

Now I will describe the application process, step by step. First, I want you to warm up by hitting shots with various clubs—short irons, longer irons, a few hybrids or fairway woods, and your driver. Be sure to pick the same target line for all of your shots. After you've warmed up, I want you to look at the ground in your hitting area. Are your divots deep or shallow? Have you not taken any divots? Are they pointed at your target, to the right of your target, or to the left? All this information—your impact conditions—will be useful in confirming your ball flight. Now study your shots to determine the category of ball-flight miss you're going to have to correct. You're going to hit three types of shots: good ones, poor ones, and terrible ones.

The good ones are the ones that are fairly solid and predictable. They might be fades, draws, high or low, slight pushes or pulls, but they will be fairly solid. Just like great golfers, your good shots won't necessarily be dead-straight bullets at the target. They won't necessarily all land on the fairway or green, but even if they don't, they'll be decent shots that are still in play. The best players don't hit every fairway or green, either. But the quality of their misses is good. That's your goal, too. You want to hit shots that leave you in a position to score. Remember, you don't have to be perfect to keep the ball in play, and that's what a good shot is—in play.

The poor ones will be hooks instead of draws, slices instead of fades, fat and thin shots, fairly big pulls or pushes. The other category, the terrible shots, can include shanks, shallow-tops, steep-tops, pop-ups, sky balls, and chops and chunks. You need to pay close attention to your poor shots and your terrible shots. They are going to tell you whether your swing DNA has developed a ball-flight miss that is too (+) or too (-). Then you'll know what you have to neutralize.

Now, for a second round of hitting, I want you to select a 6-iron and a driver. Hit 6-iron shots off the ground but hit only teed-up balls with the driver. Now aim in the same target direction as before, and every time you hit either a poor shot or a terrible shot with your 6-iron, I want you to write down what the shot did in relation to your target. Did it go right or left? Any curvature? Was it high or low, powerful or weak? Also look at any divot you might have taken. Was the divot deep or shallow, and where was it pointed? Make notes on all these things. Now hit a few drives in the same target direction. Hit enough balls to give yourself the chance to hit some poor shots and a few terrible ones. Make the same notes as you did for your 6-iron shots, although you probably won't take any divot with a teed-up driver. In fact, if you do take a divot with your driver and it's a deep hole right beneath the spot where you teed up, you can stop. You have a (+) ball-flight miss and can move on to the next step. Conversely, if you take a shallow divot before hitting a teed-up ball, then you've also unmistakably identified yourself. You have a (-) ball-flight miss. In addition to examining the ground during the 6-iron and driver tests, make a note of what your impact conditions were like during your warm-up and see if there's a consistent pattern.

Now, before you take the next step and compare your research with the ball-flight charts on pages 44–46, I want you to understand something. In all likelihood, you will have produced several different ball-flight misses. For example, you might have hit some fat shots, some thins, some pushes, and some hooks. While these are completely different shots, they are all (-) ball-flight misses. Conversely, you might have noted a number of pulls, chops and chunks, and slices. These are (+) misses. If you hit enough balls and are using both a 6-iron and a driver, you usually won't just see one miss; you'll see several different ones. Once you know you're hitting a variety of misses that are all from the same category, your next step is to look at the brief description of the ball flights you've observed and check to see if your notes on your impact conditions confirm what you've diagnosed. For example, if you keep hitting shots left of your target and your divots are fairly deep and pointed roughly where your shots went, you'll know that you're hitting pulls and not hooks (Chapter Five deals with shots that fly left of your target). I'm guessing, in addition to those pulls, that you might have hit some slices, pop-ups, and a few chunks. The deep divot and its direction will confirm this.

On the other hand, if you seldom take a divot or it's shallow and possibly behind the ball and right of your target—even just a little—then you've just confirmed a (-) ball flight. The ball flights you might have seen were pushes, hooks/slaps left (not pulls), and fats and thins.

Again, I can't stress this enough: Reading the correct ball flight and impact is so essential to correctly applying the system that if you have it wrong at this stage, you will fail. That's why I've been so long-winded and tedious in explaining all of this. You must be correct in your determination. I know what you're saying: "OK, coach, I got it. So now what?"

After identifying your ball-flight miss, you should be absolutely clear which part of your DNA is out of balance—too (+) or too (-). The next step is to read the chapters dealing with your ball-flight miss. In those chapters, I will explain the cause of your problem and offer suggestions on elements you can incorporate to fix your swing.

Now, before we go any further, I want to clear up a possible misunderstanding. I will often refer to "incorporating" an element from the opposite charts to neutralize your swing and impact. Some of you might think, "Why do I want to add more pluses or minuses to my swing when I'm already having a difficult time juggling them?" Please understand me on this: You are not adding a plus or minus to your swing when I ask you to incorporate something new. What you are actually doing is reducing a too (+) or too (-) swing flaw by neutralizing it with a swing element from the opposite side of the charts. It's just like balancing a scale. You haven't actually added a new element to your juggling act. What has occurred is that your (+) element has gotten less severe through the introduction of a (-) element into your swing. Your juggling act just got easier.

This brings me back to the start of this chapter. Remember when I said you first have to determine if you're a one- or a two-fix golfer? Well, your results after you've correctly incorporated one element will tell you. I have to give you another long-winded explanation of how this works, so please bear with me.

Your first task is to incorporate an element into your swing from the opposite category of your ball-flight miss. If your ball flight was, say, in the (-) category, you need a (+) element, and you can choose any one from the address, backswing, downswing, or impact/follow-through charts. However, when doing this, **I'd like you to go to the charts in this specific order: Start with the downswing chart. Then continue with the backswing, then the impact/follow-through chart, and finally the address charts.** This might sound strange because it's out of sequence with the order of a golf swing, but there's a good reason for this sequence. I want you to balance your swing and hit solid, reliable shots as quickly as possible, and I've found that selecting elements from the charts in this particular order will do it the quickest.

What you're trying to accomplish is a dramatic improvement in your ball flight. That doesn't mean going from a hook/slap-left (-) to a push (-) or from a slice (+) to a pull (+); those are still in the same category of ball-flight misses. You want to get back to neutral and start hitting solid and predictable shots. As an example, if you were hitting (-) ball-flight misses, then your goal is to get rid of all (-) ball flights and shift to a solid and predictable shot. If after incorporating an element from the (+) category, you still have the same ol' (-) miss, either exaggerate the element you're trying to implement or select another (+) element from the four charts. Sometimes success comes on the very next shot, but other times it takes some perseverance. Just know that you're on the right track. Getting your swing to neutral is the change you need to confirm you're a one-fix golfer.

Now let's say you incorporated a (+) element to correct your (-) ball-flight miss and you're suddenly hitting (+) misses. If that happened, you're probably a two-fix golfer. But before you jump to that conclusion, there are some things you need to check. It's possible that you misdiagnosed your original ball-flight miss and, therefore, incorporated a swing element from the same side of the charts as your miss. I'll explain how this happens by first returning to one-fix golfers and how they proceed.

As you now know, one-fix golfers need to try an element from the segments in this order: downswing, backswing, impact/follow-through, and address. When you move on to the chapters on the various ball-flight misses, you'll also find that I've made certain suggestions for elements within those swing segments that, in my experience, are the easiest and quickest ways to fix the problem. As long as you're selecting from the correct side of the charts, almost any of the elements listed will work. That's the beauty of the system—you can choose whatever elements from the correct side of the charts are the easiest for you to incorporate. You have tons of options. The only exceptions are that a slicer (+) should not incorporate a weak grip (-) or an open clubface (-). And a hooker/slap-left (-) should not incorporate a strong grip (+) or a closed clubface (+).

Whatever you choose, you need to just keep trying it until you get the desired change. You can also keep exaggerating the element until you get the desired change. For instance, if you choose to incorporate an address position where your spine angle is more to the right (-), you can exaggerate that element by bending farther and farther to the right until your ball-flight miss improves. It's that simple. Remember, the element you incorporate should produce one of two outcomes: Either your swing returns to neutral (one-fix golfer) or it shifts past neutral to a ball-flight miss on the opposite side (two-fix golfer). If you should slip back into your original ball-flight miss, just try another element or exaggerate the one you incorporated.

So what happens if one of those outcomes doesn't happen? Remember when I mentioned three paragraphs ago not to jump to the conclusion that you are a two-fix golfer until you check some things? This is where I need to insert a few words of caution for one-fix golfers. It's possible that when you try to neutralize a (+) or (-) ball flight, you'll end up with an even worse ball flight from exactly the same category you were trying to fix. Let me give you an example. Say you're hitting a hook/slap-left, which is a (-) ball-flight miss, but you misdiagnose your miss as a pull, which is a (+) miss. Since you think you're hitting a pull, you incorporate a (-) element from the charts in an effort to neutralize your swing. Big mistake. You're actually incorporating a (-) into an already (-) impact and ball flight. Now instead of improving your real problem of a hook/slap-left, you're making it worse. You will have gone from a hook/slap-left to hitting a very thin shot, which is also a (-) ball flight. If this happens, you need to stop what you're doing and go back and reevaluate your ball flight and impact. This is why I said that accurately determining your ball-flight miss is so important. If you don't catch this mistake, you might think you're a two-fix golfer instead of a one-fix golfer. You must check to make sure your initial reading is correct.

As you've already learned, you're in the two-fix golfer category if you incorporate an element to neutralize a ball-flight miss and that element shifts your ball flight past neutral to a miss on the opposite side of the chart. In the above case of mistaken identity (thinking that you're pulling shots when you're really hooking them), you might draw the conclusion that you're a two-fix golfer because incorporating a (-) to fix what you think is a pull will shift your ball-flight miss to a (-). What you should have done is incorporated a (+) to balance your true mistake of a hook/slap-left (-); this would have corrected your problem. That's why reading the ball flight and impact is so vital to proceeding correctly. Whenever in doubt, just keep hitting until you are sure of your ball flight and whether your error and DNA is a (+) or a (-).

As I mentioned earlier, about 75 to 85 percent of you are going to fall into the one-fix golfer category. But for those of you who need to incorporate two fixes into your swing, here's what you need to do. First, stop using the element you introduced into your swing when you started the process. (Although if that element came from either the downswing or impact/follow-through charts, then you might be able to use it again. But for now, put it on the shelf.)

If you recall, all two-fix golfers have a huge (+) or (-) element in the first half of their swing and an equally huge but opposite (+) or (-) in the second half of the swing. They both have to be neutralized for you to start hitting better shots, but the element you will always neutralize first will be whichever one falls in the (+) category. One-fix golfers should choose an element from a specific order of the swing-segment charts (downswing, backswing, impact/follow-through, and address). But that protocol changes for two-fix golfers. You will have to work in two segments—either the first half of the swing (address/backswing), or the second half of the swing (downswing and impact/follow-through). The segment you will always neutralize first will be the half of the swing where you have that watermelon-size (+). How will you know which half of the swing is the one with the (+)? Simple: The (+) or (-) element in the second half of the swing will always fall in the same category as the ball flight. As an example, let's say your ball flight was a hook/slap-left, which is a (-). That means you also have a big (-) element in the second half of your swing (the downswing or impact/follow-through segments). Therefore, as a two-fix golfer, that means you also have a big (+) element in the first half of your swing (address or backswing). That's the element you have to deal with first. Conversely, if you had a (+) ball-flight miss, you would know that the (+) is located in the second half of your swing, and that's the part of the swing you should deal with first.

Since you're always trying to first neutralize the plus, you'll always be selecting elements from the (-) charts as your first step. Now I want you to return to the same ball-flight chapter you were using when you started this process just like a one-fix golfer. There you will find that besides making recommendations for the one-fix golfer, I've also made selections of the elements I believe to be the easiest and most effective adjustments for the two-fix golfer. Choose from my recommendations or go to the charts and choose others and apply them just like you did before, either exaggerating the element or trying new ones until you get one to work.

If we look back to the earlier example, in which your ball-flight miss was a hook (-), you learned that the (+) you need to neutralize is in the first half of the swing. So you would use either the (-) recommendations I made for the address or backswing segments, or select your own (-) element from the charts for the same segments. You would incorporate this element, or try others, until you get a change to your ball flight. The change you'd be looking for is a very shallow/wide (-) miss. This miss will usually be a fat or thin shot, a shallow-top, or sometimes a whiff. You might not be pleased to be hitting these shots, but the good news is that this change always signals that you have neutralized the (+) in the first half of your swing. If this was your problem, I'd ask you to keep practicing that new minus (-) element for at least a couple of sessions.

Sometimes, if you keep working on it, there's a chance that the problem in the second half of the swing also will go away without the need to make any further adjustments. Why? I've seen time and time again that after a golfer neutralizes the problem in one half of the swing, particularly in the first half of the swing, the golfer's athleticism will kick in and he or she will subconsciously correct the error in the other half of the swing. So just keep practicing that first element for a while, even if you're hitting ugly shots.

If you don't correct the second swing flaw naturally, then you'll have to incorporate a second neutralizing element. In the example in which you were hooking your shots, you'll now need to incorporate a (+) element to either your downswing or impact/follow-through. The same (+) elements you might have used in the one-fix golfer process will work just fine, or you can try the ones I recommend in the proper ball-flight chapter. You can even experiment with some other elements in the (+) charts, as long as they're in the half of the swing where the (-) problem is located. You'll know which one works the best when that ugly (-) ball flight turns into a neutral ball flight.

I know when you read this for the first time that it can be confusing and hard to digest in its entirety. So to make things easier, let me give you a summary of how to apply the system.

STEP 1: Diagnose your ball-flight miss and confirm it with the impact conditions. Then check the charts to see if your swing DNA is too (+) or too (-). Remember to pick out the miss from the (+) or (-) charts that you seem to hit the most often. Then study the chapter devoted to that particular ball flight.

STEP 2: Go to the end of that ball-flight chapter and incorporate either one of the recommended elements to fix the problem or any one of the other elements from the four swing-segment charts that suits you. The recommended order of selection from the charts is downswing, backswing, impact/follow-through, and address. Then keep trying different elements, or exaggerate a specific element, until your ball flight changes.

STEP 3: If your ball flight changed to one that is neutral, solid, and easily repeatable, you're a one-fix golfer and are done with this process. You might take a step backward from time to time and produce this ball-flight miss again, but now you know how to correct it. If your ball flight changed to a miss on the opposite side of the plus/minus chart from your original problem, continue to Step 4.

STEP 4: Reconfirm that you've correctly applied the system. There are several mistakes you could have made, including misdiagnosing your ball-flight miss or choosing elements to incorporate from the wrong charts.

STEP 5: Assuming that you've reconfirmed your miss, identify the location of the large (+) element in your swing. It will be in either the first half of the swing (address or backswing) or in the second half (downswing, impact/follow-through). The key to finding it is knowing that your ball-flight miss will always be in the same (+) or (-) category as the second half of your swing. Neutralize the (+) element, wherever it's located, by incorporating a (-) from the charts that deal with the corresponding half of the swing. You'll know you did this process correctly if you develop a bad (-) ball-flight miss such as thins, fats, or shallow-tops.

STEP 6: Practice the (-) element you've incorporated into the swing for at least two sessions. The new (-) ball-flight miss might disappear and turn into a solid and repeatable neutral ball flight. If that happens, you're done. If it doesn't, go to Step 7.

STEP 7: Incorporate either a recommended (+) element or one from the corresponding half of the swing where the large (-) element resides. Exaggerate this element or try others until your ball flight becomes neutral, solid, and repeatable. Now you're done.

FINAL THOUGHTS: Once you start hitting good, solid, and predictable shots, whether you're a one- or a two-fix golfer, you're at neutral. The shots might be a little low or high, a slight push or pull, or a fade or a draw, but they will be solid and predictable. You're now seeing your natural ball flight. You might be a Lee Trevino with a slightly low push fade, but you'll be solid and predictable. Conversely, you might be hitting high draws like Tom Watson, but once again, you'll be solid and predictable. Now you can enjoy the game more and score better, because you can plan your shots.

The great thing about this book is that whether you're in the one-fix or two-fix category, there are many options for neutralizing the out-of-balance pluses and minuses in your swing. You can just keep trying different things in the various charts—as long as they're in the same (+) or (-) category and the correct swing segment—until you find the swing elements that really click. Most of them will work, but you might not be comfortable with one adjustment versus another. That's why I explained in the introduction that teaching a specific swing method doesn't make sense for most players. We all learn differently, and it takes a good teacher—in this case, you—to figure out how to get the lesson to really sink in.

I've used these first three chapters to explain in detail my plus/minus system and how it works in terms of improving your golf swing and ball flight. In the following chapters, I will give you step-by-step instructions on how to use this book to understand your swing DNA by correctly reading your ball-flight miss. I will go over each miss in detail, so that you can correctly identify it. I'll also give you information about the impact conditions that will let you confirm the ball flight. Finally, I'll give you some recommendations on the (+) or (-) swing elements you might try for each ball-flight miss. These recommendations come from all my years of teaching. I've found them to be the easiest and most effective way to neutralize the problems we all suffer from.

BALL-FLIGHT MISSES

PLUS (+) Steep or narrow

PULL: Ball flies on a straight path left of target (often a deep divot pointing left of target).

SLICE: Ball curves right of target. Curve might be only slight. (Sizeable divot pointed left of ball's flight.)

CHOP/CHUNK: Ball flies shorter than the distance the club is capable of producing. Tee shots are often popped up (deep divot starting at or behind the ball's position at address and likely pointing left of target).

TOE HIT: Ball travels shorter than the distance the club is capable of producing. Falls out of the sky due to lack of backspin. Direction of ball is unpredictable but often to the right of target with irons and curving to the left with a driver or fairway wood. (Instead of looking at the ground, check the club. There will either be a ball mark out toward the toe of the club or, if the ball was teed up, evidence of tee marks out toward the toe on the bottom of the club.)

STEEP-TOP: Ball runs along the ground, often taking big hops (no evidence of a divot or, on occasion, very deep divots at the ball's location at address).

STEEP-TRAP: Ball either flies on low trajectory, or doesn't get off the ground when using lower-lofted clubs. Usually goes left of your target and can be produced with any club except shorter irons, especially wedges (deep divot pointing left of your target).

HIGH-STEEP: Ball flies excessively high on short-iron shots, or is popped up when the ball is teed up and struck with a driver or fairway wood. (Deep divots with irons off the ground. Marks on the top part of the face or the top of woods when the ball is teed up. Also look for broken tees and a possible divot.)

MINUS (-) Shallow or wide

PUSH: Ball flies on a straight path right of your target (no divot or shallow divot pointing right of target, on line with ball's path).

HOOK/SLAP-LEFT: Ball flies left of your target with varying amounts of curvature (shallow divot or no divot; divot always points to the right of the ball flight).

FATS/THINS: Ball flies shorter than the distance the club is capable of producing, but at various trajectories (shallow divot behind the ball's position at address, usually pointing right of the target or at the target, or no evidence of a divot).

HEEL/SHANK: Ball travels shorter than the distance the club is capable of producing. With a driver or fairway wood, will curve to the right and float in the air with too much backspin. With an iron, will likely fly straight right and lower than normal. (Instead of looking at the ground, check the club. There will either be a ball mark close to the heel of the club or, if the ball was teed up, tee marks on the heel or shaft side of the middle part of the club's sole.)

SHALLOW-TOP: Ball runs along the ground, often in a skipping motion (no evidence of a divot, or a very shallow divot well behind the ball's location at address).

LOW-SHALLOW: Ball flies on a low trajectory and travels shorter than the distance the club is capable of delivering. Typically produced with less-lofted fairway woods and longer irons off the ground (very shallow divot behind ball's position at address or no evidence of divot).

HIGH-SHALLOW: Ball flies nearly straight up in the air only with high-lofted irons off the ground. Can be hit when the ball is teed up (shallow divot behind the ball, or none at all).

PLUS AND MINUS CORRECTION CHARTS

Address

PLUS (+)		MINUS (-)	
Body	**Arms & Club**	**Body**	**Arms & Club**
1. Bend spine over more	1. Grip stronger	1. Set spine more upright	1. Grip weaker
2. Move head and hips left, put more weight on left leg	2. Lean handle ahead of ball	2. Tilt spine to right, put more weight on right leg	2. Set handle even with clubhead
3. Stand closer to ball		3. Stand farther from ball	
4. Open shoulders to hips		4. Close shoulders to hips	

Backswing

PLUS (+)		MINUS (-)	
Body	**Arms & Club**	**Body**	**Arms & Club**
1. Prevent head move to right, put more weight on left leg	1. Swing arms, club more upright (plane)	1. Let head move to right, put more weight on right leg	1. Flatten arm, club swing (plane)
2. Steepen shoulder turn	2. Swing arms, club straighter back (direction)	2. Flatten shoulder turn	2. Swing arms, club more inside (direction)
3. Restrict hip turn	3. Point shaft more to right at top (across the line)	3. Make bigger hip, shoulder turn	3. Extend arms wider, cock wrists less, point club more left
4. Increase/lower spine		4. Raise spine	

Downswing

PLUS (+)		MINUS (-)	
Body	**Arms & Club**	**Body**	**Arms & Club**
1. Increase/lower spine	1. Close clubface	1. Raise spine	1. Open clubface
2. Turn shoulders, hips around and to left	2. Swing arms more left, toward out-to-in	2. Thrust right hip at ball, restrict shoulder turn	2. Swing arms, club more in-to-out
3. Move entire body more toward target, onto left leg		3. Slide hips toward target, tilt shoulders behind ball	

Impact/Follow-through

PLUS (+)		MINUS (-)	
Body	**Arms & Club**	**Body**	**Arms & Club**
1. Finish with upper body directly over lower body, 100 percent of weight on left leg	1. Swing arms, club handle more left	1. Finish with upper body behind lower body, some weight on right leg	1. Swing arms, club more in-to-out, right of target line
2. Make bigger shoulder, hip turn around to left	2. Close clubface	2. Restrict shoulder, hip turn	2. Open, block clubface
	3. Lean shaft forward		3. Set handle even with clubhead at impact
	4. Swing more down on ball		4. Swing more up on ball

DEFINITIONS

Address Terms

INCREASE/LOWER SPINE:
Bending over more from the
hips so that the top of the spine
is closer to the ground.

**MOVE HEAD, HIPS LEFT; PUT
MORE WEIGHT ON LEFT LEG:**
Leaning the entire body slightly
toward the target.

STAND CLOSER TO BALL:
Shaft position is more vertical.

OPEN SHOULDERS TO HIPS:
Shoulders aligned slightly left
of the target while hips aligned
parallel with the target.

GRIP STRONGER:
Hands positioned
on club so that the
creases created
by the thumb and
forefinger of each
hand point right of
chin, toward right
shoulder.

LEAN HANDLE FORWARD OF BALL:
The top of the golf shaft is angled
closer to the target than
the bottom of the shaft.

SET SPINE MORE UPRIGHT:
Spine is more perpendicular to ground, with less hip hinge.

TILT SPINE TO RIGHT, PUT MORE WEIGHT ON RIGHT LEG:
Leaning the upper torso away from the target, with left shoulder higher than the right.

STAND FARTHER FROM BALL:
Increasing distance from ball so
clubshaft is more parallel to ground.

CLOSE SHOULDERS TO HIPS:
Shoulders aligned slightly right
of the target while hips are
aligned parallel with the target.

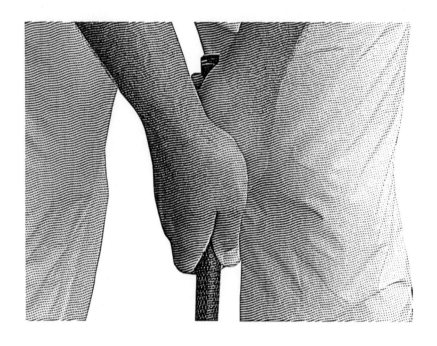

GRIP WEAKER:
Hands positioned on the club so that
the creases created by the thumb and
forefinger of each hand are pointing
toward the chin.

SET HANDLE EVEN WITH CLUBHEAD:
The shaft handle, when viewed from face
on, is even with or just behind the ball.

Backswing Terms

PREVENT HEAD MOVE TO RIGHT, PUT MORE WEIGHT ON LEFT LEG: Keeping the head still and centered over the ball while preventing any lateral movement with the hips to the right, away from the target, so that the weight in the lower body is on the left leg.

STEEPEN SHOULDER TURN: The left shoulder is noticeably closer to the ground than the right when the shoulder turn is completed.

RESTRICT HIP TURN:
Hips remain fairly still and
aligned with the target while
the shoulders turn back.

INCREASE/LOWER SPINE:
Bending over more from the
hips so that the top of the spine
is closer to the ground.

SWING ARMS, CLUB MORE UPRIGHT:
Arms swing the club back on a steeper
angle toward the sky.

**SWING ARMS, CLUB
STRAIGHTER BACK:**
Arms initially take the
club back along the
target line.

**POINT SHAFT MORE TO RIGHT
AT TOP (ACROSS THE LINE):**
At the top of the backswing,
the shaft is pointing right of the
target.

**LET HEAD MOVE TO RIGHT, PUT
MORE WEIGHT ON RIGHT LEG:**
Allow head to move off the ball
away from the target, so that the
chin is pointing behind the ball's
position, while shifting more
weight onto the right leg.

FLATTEN SHOULDER TURN:
While turning in the backswing,
the left and right shoulders are
more level to the ground.

MAKE BIGGER HIP, SHOULDER TURN:
The torso rotates as far as possible
away from the target.

RAISE SPINE:
Standing taller so the spine is more
upright than at address.

FLATTEN ARM, CLUB SWING:
Arms and clubshaft move lower
and more around the body, more
parallel to the ground.

SWING ARMS, CLUB MORE INSIDE:
Arms and club move back inside
the target line.

EXTEND ARMS WIDER, COCK WRISTS
LESS, POINT CLUB MORE LEFT:
Maintaining extension in arms, delaying
any wrist cock as long as possible, and
pointing shaft left of the target at the
top.

Downswing Terms

INCREASE/LOWER SPINE:
Bending over more from the hips so that the top of the spine is closer to the ground.

TURN SHOULDERS, HIPS AROUND TO LEFT:
Shoulders and hips turn together, opening to the target, and the club swings more on a path from out-to-in.

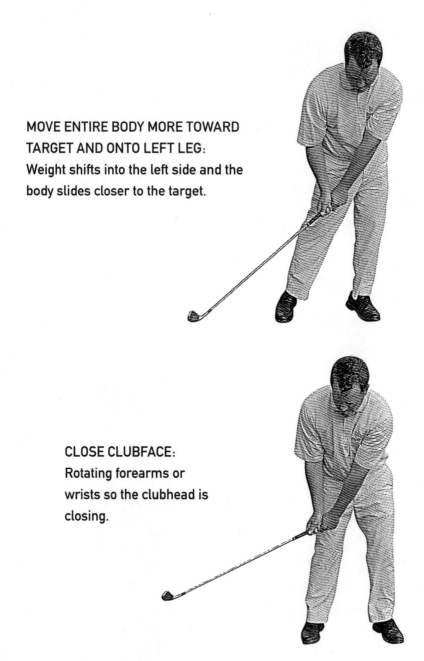

MOVE ENTIRE BODY MORE TOWARD
TARGET AND ONTO LEFT LEG:
Weight shifts into the left side and the
body slides closer to the target.

CLOSE CLUBFACE:
Rotating forearms or
wrists so the clubhead is
closing.

**SWING ARMS MORE LEFT,
TOWARD OUT-TO-IN:**
Arms and club move from
outside the target line toward
inside the target line.

RAISE SPINE:
Standing taller so the spine
is more upright.

**THRUST RIGHT HIP AT BALL,
RESTRICT SHOULDER TURN:**
Start the downswing with a
movement of the right hip
outward and forward toward the
ball while holding your shoulders
from turning back toward the
target.

**SLIDE HIPS TOWARD TARGET,
TILT SHOULDERS BEHIND BALL:**
Bump hips out toward the target
while the top of the spine and
your head move away from it
with right shoulder lowering and
left shoulder rising.

OPEN CLUBFACE:
Rotate club clockwise so clubface is opening.

SWING ARMS, CLUB MORE IN-TO-OUT:
Arms and clubshaft move down from inside the target line toward outside the line.

Impact/Follow-through Terms

FINISH WITH UPPER BODY DIRECTLY OVER LOWER, 100 PERCENT WEIGHT ON LEFT LEG: Supporting body weight entirely with the left leg through impact and finishing with torso aligned straight up and down.

MAKE BIGGER HIP, SHOULDER TURN AROUND TO LEFT: Shoulders and hips turn together, opening to the target, and the club swings more on a path from out-to-in.

SWING ARMS, CLUB HANDLE MORE LEFT: Arms and club handle move through impact on an out-to-in path.

CLOSE CLUBFACE: Rotating the forearms or wrists so that the clubhead is closing and facing left of the target after impact.

LEAN SHAFT FORWARD:
Handle of the club is leaning
closer to the target than the
clubhead when the ball is
struck.

SWING MORE DOWN ON BALL:
Club strikes the ball from a
steeper angle of attack.

FINISH WITH UPPER BODY
BEHIND LOWER BODY, SOME
WEIGHT ON RIGHT LEG:
Legs and hips closer to
the target than the chest,
shoulders, and head, while
supporting some body weight
with the right leg.

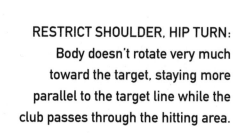

RESTRICT SHOULDER, HIP TURN:
Body doesn't rotate very much
toward the target, staying more
parallel to the target line while the
club passes through the hitting area.

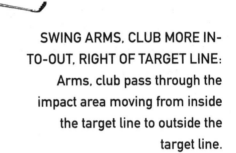

SWING ARMS, CLUB MORE IN-TO-OUT, RIGHT OF TARGET LINE: Arms, club pass through the impact area moving from inside the target line to outside the target line.

OPEN, BLOCK CLUBFACE: Rotating the forearms or wrists clockwise so that the clubhead points right of the target through impact and the clubhead does not pass the grip until well after impact.

SET HANDLE EVEN WITH CLUBHEAD AT IMPACT:
The head of the club is allowed to swing past the club handle so that the clubshaft is not leading the clubhead through impact.

SWING MORE UP ON BALL:
Striking the ball on an ascending path.

Chapter Four

BALL-FLIGHT MISSES THAT FLY RIGHT OF YOUR TARGET

There are two common ball-flight misses that fly right of your target—the slice and the push. I'm sure most of you are aware of the slice. It is, by far, the most common ball-flight miss in golf, and I'm guessing that you've hit at least a few over the years. The slice, by definition, occurs when a ball flies on a curving path to the right of your target (left for left-handers). Sometimes a slice starts left of your target and then curves back to the right. Sometimes it starts on your target line and curves to the right. And sometimes it starts right of your target but curves even farther right of your target. Finally, because today's clubs minimize sidespin, you might even hit a slice to the right that doesn't curve much at all. In other words, there are more than a few versions. But the universally common element is that your ball curves to the right because the clubface is open in relation to its path. Any time your ball goes to the right of the direction of your divot, it's a slice ball-flight miss. I should also make it clear that the slice is the big brother of the "fade," which is the commonly used term for a ball that only curves a little, and sometimes hardly at all, to the right. The fade, unlike the slice, is *not* what I'd consider a ball-flight miss. It's a controlled and intentional curving of the golf ball. In fact, many golfers make a career out of playing a fade. If you go from slicing the ball to hitting a solid shot that fades, and it's a ball flight that you can repeat, then you've certainly met the goal of this book.

A push is often confused with a slice. An even more common mistake is that some golfers think a slice and a push are caused by the same swing elements. They are not. A push is any shot that flies on a straight line right of your target. In other words, the ball doesn't curve at all, but it starts right and stays right. It's also sometimes referred to as a "block," because the golfer's body blocks the club from swinging on the ideal in-to-in path. While a slice is typically a weak hit, the push is usually well struck. It's the type of miss that better players often have, and it occurs when the clubface is square to a clubpath that moves from inside to outside the target line. In fact, when I spoke in earlier chapters about hitting solid shots with a reliable ball flight, a slight push would certainly fall in this category. But I want to make it clear that a full-blown push is definitely a ball-flight miss, and this chapter will help you reduce or eliminate it.

Now that you know the difference between the two shots, let's first work on curing a slice. If you refer to the charts, you'll see that all slices are a (+) ball-flight miss. It's not a particularly powerful shot for three reasons: (1) it's a glancing blow, because the clubface is open to your path at impact; (2) the steep (+) angle of approach means that much of the swing's energy is lost in the ground, instead of being delivered into the back of the ball; and (3) the combination of an open face and a steep angle of approach adds loft and spin to the ball flight.

You'll be able to verify that you sliced the shot by checking the ground where your ball was sitting at address. The impact condition you'll most often see is a fairly deep divot that is pointing left of your ball flight. Or, if you teed up a driver or a fairway wood, you'll often see the ball pop up in the air and the tee broken or knocked out of the ground. The impact is actually a combination of (+) and (-) elements.

It's classified as a (+) because the initial error causing the shot is too many pluses in your swing, but the (-) comes into play because of the open clubface at impact. The degree of steep/narrow (+) in any slice depends on how much the clubface is open at impact. The more it's open, the bigger the slice. But that also means the swing sometimes might not be as steep/narrow (+) and the divot might not be as deep. With the driver, the more the face is open, the more your ball will slice, but you might not hit a pop-up. Conversely, if the clubface isn't open that much, the ball won't slice as much, but the swing will have a greater degree of steep/narrow elements and the ball could pop up.

If you're slicing the ball, there's a 50 percent chance you're a one-fix golfer. If you are, then your slice can be eliminated entirely or turned into a solid, manageable fade. If you still want to get rid of that fade, just make a second adjustment and strengthen your grip at address or close the clubface in the downswing after you have taken the first step of neutralizing your steep (+) swing. The reason the one-fix golfer might have to make this second adjustment is because of the combination of (+) and (-) elements I mentioned earlier. You swing down into the ball too steeply (+) and compensate for that by opening the clubface at impact (-). With a steep approach like this, you have to open the face to get the ball airborne. So, in order for you to fix a slice, you first have to correct the steep angle, and then you might also have to fix the compensation move of an open clubface.

You can pick any one (-) element from the four charts to fix a slice, except for weakening your grip or opening the clubface at impact. Those two won't work, since the face already is open and might need to be dealt with later. Here are some of my (-) recommendations. Remember to try them in the prescribed order of the charts I list here (downswing, backswing, impact/follow-through, address).

- **DURING THE DOWNSWING:** 1. Thrust your right hip toward the ball; 2. Swing your arms and club down and in-to-out.
- **DURING THE BACKSWING:** 1. Make a flatter swing with your arms and club; 2. Make a bigger shoulder and hip turn.
- **DURING IMPACT/FOLLOW-THROUGH:** 1. Restrict your shoulder and hip turn; 2. Swing your arms and club more in-to-out to the right of the target line.
- **AT ADDRESS:** 1. Tilt your spine to the right with more weight on your right foot; 2. Close your shoulders in relation to your hips.

Any one of those (-) elements should do the trick, but feel free to try others from the four charts (except for weakening your grip or opening the clubface) if you don't feel comfortable with those adjustments. I should also add that you can try incorporating more than one of these elements if your slices are really bad. It's just like adding more weight to one side of a scale to get it to balance out.

Now, as I mentioned above, you might also have to deal with the compensation move of an open clubface (-). You need a (+) to get rid of it, and I'd recommend one of the following:

- **AT ADDRESS:** Take a stronger grip.
- **DURING THE DOWNSWING:** Close the clubface.
- **DURING IMPACT/FOLLOW-THROUGH:** Close the clubface.

By first incorporating at least one (-) to your swing and then incorporating a (+) to correct the open clubface compensation, you should be slice-free.

Now let's deal with those of you who fall into the two-fix category. Just like the one-fix golfers who sometimes have to make two adjustments to correct the path and the open clubface, a two-fix golfer might have to make three adjustments—two fixes, and then a third one to change the grip or close the club in the downswing. The third one should be made last and only if the slice hasn't been fixed. If you are a two-fix slicer, then you have a very (-) shallow/wide element in the first half of your swing and you compensate in the second half with a (+) so you can make contact with the ball. The compensation is usually swinging on an out-to-in path during the downswing and impact/follow-through segments.

You'll know you're in the two-fix category after you start the process like a one-fix golfer and incorporate a (-) element.

When you do, your ball-flight miss will go from a (+) to a (-). You'll probably hit a shallow-top or a thin shot, which are very wide/shallow (-) misses.

So what do you do now? Like all two-fix golfers, your first step is to locate and neutralize the watermelon-size (+) element. It's either in the first half of your swing or the second. How do you know which? Your ball-flight miss is always the same as the dominant element in the second half of your swing. Since a slice is a (+) ball flight, you know the big (+) you have to neutralize is in the second half. So you should apply a (-) from either the downswing or impact/follow-through chart.

As soon as this happens, your ball flight will be a very shallow/wide (-) miss, even to the point of hitting tops or missing the ball entirely. Keep practicing this new element.

Sometimes, your natural athleticism will correct the ball-flight issue without you having to make any further adjustments. But after at least two sessions, if your slice isn't cured, you will now need to incorporate a steep/narrow (+) element into the first half of your swing from either the address or backswing chart.

Here's the process and some elements I'd recommend trying.

- **DURING THE DOWNSWING:** 1. Swing on a more in-to-out path; 2. Thrust your right hip at the ball.
- **DURING IMPACT/FOLLOW-THROUGH:** 1. Swing more in-to-out and to the right of your target line; 2. Restrict your hip and shoulder turn to the left.

If you're not comfortable with these, you can try any (-) elements from the downswing or impact/follow-through charts except opening the clubface, which will exacerbate the slice.

Once you've incorporated that (-) element, now it's time to fix the (-) problem in the first half of the swing. I have some recommendations.

- **AT ADDRESS:** Bend your spine over more.
- **DURING THE BACKSWING:** 1. Get the shaft of your club pointing more to the right of your target at the top (across the line); 2. Swing your arms and club more upright.

Finally, if your open clubface is still a problem and the slice persists, you are going to have to strengthen your grip at address or close the clubface in the downswing.

SLICE CHECKLIST

BALL-FLIGHT MISS: (+)

FLIGHT DESCRIPTION: Curves right of your target. The curve might be a lot or only slight.

IMPACT CONDITION: Noticeable divot pointing left of your ball flight.

CAUSE: Clubface is open to the path at impact.

ONE-FIX GOLFER: Incorporate one (-) element from the prescribed chart order of downswing, backswing, impact/ follow-through, address (except strengthening your grip or closing the clubface). Note: If your ball-flight miss doesn't improve, and instead changes to a (-), go to the instructions for the two-fix golfer.

RECOMMENDATIONS FOR THE ONE-FIX GOLFER: Downswing: thrust right hip toward ball; swing arms, club down and in-to-out. Backswing: make a flatter arms and club swing; or make a bigger shoulder and hip turn. Impact/ follow-through: restrict shoulder, hip turn; or swing arms, club more in-to-out to right of target line. Address: tilt spine to right with more weight on right foot; close shoulders in relation to hips. If slice persists, Address: employ stronger grip. Downswing: close clubface.

TWO-FIX GOLFER: Incorporate one minus (-) element from downswing or impact/follow-through chart. If after practicing it for a while your miss doesn't improve to a neutral ball flight, incorporate a plus (+) element from address or backswing chart.

RECOMMENDATIONS FOR THE TWO-FIX GOLFER: Fix No. 1—Downswing: swing arms, club more in-to-out; thrust right hip at ball. Impact/follow-through: swing arms, club more in-to-out to right of target line; or restrict hip, shoulder turn to left. Fix No. 2—Address: bend spine over more. Backswing: point shaft more right of target at top (across the line); swing arms, club more upright. If slice persists, Fix No. 3—Address: employ stronger grip. Downswing: close clubface.

Now let's deal with the push. First, check your ball flight. You're hitting pushes if your ball flies on a straight line right of your target. The path might be slightly right of your target or considerably right, but there will be no curvature. The trajectory is typically low with fairway woods and long irons and higher with short irons. This is a (-) ball-flight miss.

Now check your impact conditions. Remember, the ball goes straight right because the clubface was square to an in-to-out swing path at impact. You'll most often notice a very shallow divot or no evidence of a divot. There could also be a shallow divot behind the ball as a result of skimming the ground before impact. If there is a divot, it will be pointed to the right of the target and on the ball's path. The push's ball flight is always in the direction of the swing path at impact. Even if contact is made with the ground before the ball, this is still a fairly powerful shot and is a common miss for better players, even tour pros.

The push will most often fall into the one-fix category. Sometimes, however, a push can be the product of being too steep at the top of the backswing and then shallowing things out in the second half of the swing with an in-to-out path. If that's what you're doing, then you're a two-fix golfer.

If you're a one-fix golfer, you need to incorporate a (+) element into your swing to neutralize your fault of having too many (-) elements. Although you can choose any (+) element you feel comfortable with, here are my recommendations. Remember to try them from the prescribed order of charts.

> **DURING THE DOWNSWING:** 1. Turn your shoulders and hips to the left; 2. Swing arms more left toward out-to-in.
> **DURING THE BACKSWING:** 1. Swing your arms straighter back and more down the target line; 2. Restrict your hip turn.
> **DURING THE IMPACT/FOLLOW-THROUGH:** 1. Swing your arms and the club handle more to the left of your target; 2. Turn your shoulders and hips more to the left.
> **AT ADDRESS:** 1. Stand closer to the ball; 2. Open your shoulders in relation to your hips.

If after incorporating a (+), you're now hitting slices, pulls, or even steep-chops—all (+) ball-flight misses—then your push needs two fixes. Your problem is that you have a watermelon-size (+) element dominating the first half of your swing and you compensate for it by being too (-) in the second half.

Like all two-fix golfers, your first step is to neutralize the watermelon-size (+) element. You know it's in the first half of your swing because your ball-flight miss is always the same as the dominant element in the second half of your swing. Since a push is a (-) ball flight, then you know the big (+) is not in the second half.

Incorporate a (-) element from either the address or backswing charts to neutralize the too (+) nature of the first half of your swing. You can choose from several elements, but I have some recommendations.

> **AT ADDRESS:** Tilt your spine more to the right and put more weight on your right leg.
> **DURING THE BACKSWING:** 1. Make a flatter arm and club swing; 2. Make a bigger hip and shoulder turn.

Once you've incorporated a (-) in the first half of your swing, you'll now start hitting shots that have a very (-) ball flight. You'll see thins and even shallow-tops. Now you need to steepen (+) the second half of your swing to get rid of the compensation move. Again, I have some recommendations:

> **DURING THE DOWNSWING:** 1. Move your entire body, head, and hips more toward the target and shift your weight onto your left leg; 2. Swing your arms more to the left toward out-to-in.
> **DURING IMPACT/FOLLOW-THROUGH:** 1. Swing your arms and the handle of the club more to the left; 2. Turn your hips and shoulders more to the left.

Remember, my recommendations might not necessarily be the easiest for you, so feel free to try others if these don't click.

PUSH CHECKLIST

BALL-FLIGHT MISS: (-)

FLIGHT DESCRIPTION: Right of your target with no curve. Low trajectory with fairway woods and long irons, high trajectory with high-lofted irons.

IMPACT CONDITION: Shallow divot pointing right of your target on line with ball flight, or no evidence of a divot.

CAUSE: Swing path at impact is in-to-out with the clubface square to the path.

ONE-FIX GOLFER: Incorporate one (+) element from the prescribed chart order of downswing, backswing, impact/follow-through, address. Note: If your ball-flight miss doesn't improve, and instead changes to a (+), go to the instructions for the two-fix golfer.

RECOMMENDATIONS FOR THE ONE-FIX GOLFER: Downswing: turn hips, shoulders more left; swing arms more left toward out-to-in. Backswing: swing arms straighter back, more down the target line; restrict hip turn. Impact/follow-through: swing arms, club handle more to left of target; turn shoulders, hips more left. Address: stand closer to ball or open shoulders in relation to hips.

TWO-FIX GOLFER: Incorporate a (-) element from either address or backswing chart. If after some practice your ball-flight miss doesn't dramatically improve, then incorporate a (+) from downswing or impact/follow-through chart.

RECOMMENDATIONS FOR THE TWO-FIX GOLFER: Fix No. 1—Address: tilt spine more to right, put more weight on right leg. Backswing: make flatter arm, club swing; or make bigger hip, shoulder turn. Fix No. 2—Downswing: move body, head, hips more toward target and onto left leg; or swing arms more left toward out-to-in. Impact/follow-through: swing arms, club handle more left; or turn hips, shoulders more left.

Chapter Five

BALL-FLIGHT MISSES THAT FLY LEFT OF YOUR TARGET

J ust as the slice and push (see Chapter Four) cover the majority of ball-flight misses that are right of the target, the pull and hook/slap-left cover the same territory left of the target. The pull is a shot that flies on a straight line left of the target, while the hook and slap-left are similar but slightly different shots in which the ball curves left of the path you are swinging on at impact. For the purposes of fixing your swing, consider the hook and slap-left as the same ball-flight miss, but I'll explain the difference.

If you excessively rotate your wrists and forearms counterclockwise through impact, you will hit a hook. The rotation closes the clubface relative to the path, causing sidespin, and forces contact with the ball closer to its equator, which increases the sidespin and produces the curve to the left. The slap-left is also caused by closing the clubface, but instead of the forearms and wrists rolling over to achieve this, the face shuts with a slapping motion of your right hand, causing the ball to travel left. The club is not delofted, so the ball is struck lower on its surface, causing more backspin, and doesn't come off with as much sidespin. Thus, the curvature of a slap-left is sometimes so subtle that people will often confuse it with a pull. In fact, advances in equipment have reduced the curve of a hook, so that it can also be mistaken for a pull. But the telltale difference between a hook/slap-left and a pull is that a hook/slap-left will always fly left of your path. It might not curve all that much, but if it's left of your path, it's a hook/slap-left. I should also make it clear that the hook/slap-left is the big brother of the "draw," which is the commonly used term for a ball that only curves a little—and sometimes hardly at all—to the left. The draw, unlike the hook, is not what I'd consider a ball-flight miss. It's a controlled and intentional curving of the golf ball. In fact, many golfers make a career out of playing a draw.

The hook/slap-left is also usually the product of a swing path that comes from inside your target line on the downswing but moves outside your target line or down your target line through impact. The trajectory of the shot and severity of the curvature depend on the position of the clubface in relation to the path. The more delofted and closed it is, the lower the ball will typically fly and the more it will curve. Even though the hook/slap-left is considered a glancing blow, it's a fairly powerful shot for two reasons: (1) the in-to-out path and the in-to-down-the-line path that are typical of this ball flight are both shallow/wide (-) angles of attack, which puts power into the side of the ball instead of the ground; (2) the club is in a normal or strengthened loft position. The delofted shot tends to bore through the air with less back-spin. And once it hits the ground, it typically rolls instead of checking up. It's usually a better player's miss, because most higher-handicap amateurs swing down into the ball on the opposite path: out-to-in.

To verify either a hook or a slap-left, look and see if you've made a divot. There's often no divot because the hook/slap-left is a shallow impact and ball flight (-). But if you've been hitting several shots from the same place, sooner or later you'll probably make a divot. Check its direction. If the ball flew left of the divot, then you've hit a hook/slap-left. If the divot is left of your target but it's pointing roughly on the same line that the ball flew, then you've hit a pull. A hook/slap-left is typically a better player's problem, is often accompanied by a push, and is a (-) ball flight.

Most golfers who hit this shot need one fix to correct the problem. If this is you, incorporate a (+) element into your swing. Any of the (+) elements will work except employing a stronger grip or closing the clubface, as these contribute to the hook. Instead, I have some recommendations, but remember to try them in the prescribed order of the charts I list here (downswing, backswing, impact/follow-through, address).

- DURING THE DOWNSWING: 1. Turn your shoulders and hips more around and to the left; 2. Swing your arms more to the left toward out-to-in.
- DURING THE BACKSWING: 1. Restrict your hip turn; 2. Swing your arms and club straighter back.
- IMPACT/FOLLOW-THROUGH: 1. Swing your arms and club handle more to the left of your target; 2. Lean the handle forward.
- AT ADDRESS: Put more weight on your left leg.

After doing this, you might now be hitting a draw, which is a neutral ball flight that curves slightly to the left. This is not a ball-flight miss, but if you wish to get rid of it, either weaken your grip at address or open the clubface during impact/follow-through. Remember not to make any grip adjustment until you have neutralized the hook/slap-left (-), otherwise you won't neutralize your ball flight.

Now let's say that after incorporating one of the (+) items above, you then develop a (+) ball-flight miss. You're a two-fix golfer. You have a watermelon-size (+) element in the first half of your swing, so you've been compensating by making a big (-) move in the second half of your swing, and that's causing you to hit hooks.

What do you do? First, neutralize the (+) element. You know it's in the first half of your swing and not the second half, because your original ball-flight miss was a (-), and that always matches up with the dominant element in the second half. When you incorporate a (-) from the address or backswing charts, your ball-flight miss will likely become very (-). You'll probably start hitting shallow-tops or even miss the ball completely. Sometimes you can intuitively correct the problem, but if after practicing for at least two or three sessions you don't start hitting good, solid shots instead of those tops and whiffs, you're going to have to neutralize this (-) element, too.

Now let me give you the recommended steps and elements for the two-fix golfer.

- **AT ADDRESS:** Tilt your spine more to the right with more weight on your right leg.
- **DURING THE BACKSWING:** 1. Extend your arms wider with less wrist cock; 2. Make a flatter arm and club swing.

Practice this for a while. If things don't improve, here are my recommendations for Step 2.

- DURING THE DOWNSWING: 1. Turn your shoulders and hips more around to the left; 2. Swing your arms and club more to the left toward out-to-in.
- DURING IMPACT/FOLLOW-THROUGH: 1. Swing your arms and the club handle more to the left; 2. Lean the shaft forward.

If you're now hitting solid shots but still have a slight curve in your ball flight, you can get rid of it by either weakening your grip or opening the clubface through impact.

HOOK/SLAP-LEFT CHECKLIST

BALL-FLIGHT MISS: (-)

FLIGHT DESCRIPTION: Flies left of your target with varying amounts of curvature.

IMPACT CONDITION: Shallow divot or no divot; always pointing to the right of the ball flight.

CAUSE: Clubface is facing left of the club's path at impact.

ONE-FIX GOLFER: Incorporate one (+) element from the prescribed order of downswing, backswing, impact/ follow-through, address charts, except strengthening your grip or closing the clubface. Note: If your ball-flight miss doesn't improve, and instead changes to a (+), go to the instructions for the two-fix golfer.

RECOMMENDATIONS FOR THE ONE-FIX GOLFER: Downswing: turn shoulders, hips around and to left; or swing arms more left toward out-to-in. Backswing: restrict hip turn; or swing arms, club straighter back. Impact/follow-

through: swing arms, club handle more left of target; or lean shaft forward. Address: put more weight on left leg.
TWO-FIX GOLFER: Incorporate one (-) element from the address or backswing charts. If, after some practice, your shots don't dramatically improve, then incorporate one (+) element from the downswing or impact/follow-through charts.
RECOMMENDATIONS FOR THE TWO-FIX GOLFER: Fix No. 1—Address: tilt spine more right, put more weight on right leg; or weaken grip. Backswing: extend arms wider with less wrist cock; or make flatter arm, club swing. Fix No. 2—Downswing: turn shoulders, hips more around to left; swing arms, club more left toward out-to-in. Impact/follow-through: swing arms, club handle more left; or lean shaft forward.

Now let's fix the pull. As I said earlier, you'll know you're hitting a pull if your ball flies left of your target without curving and your divot is pointed in the same direction. Most of the time, the pull (+) is not a powerful shot, because your swing path, which moves from outside the target line on the downswing to inside the target line through impact, is steep, and too much power is lost when the club hits the ground. The pull is a common ball-flight miss for higher handicappers because they approach the ball on a very steep/narrow out-to-in path (+). The shot is an exaggerated miss when the golfer is swinging a driver, because a driver requires a shallow/wide angle of approach to hit the ball solidly. The steep/narrow path will cause most driver shots to either pop up or fly way shorter than normal due to too much backspin. It should also be noted that the pull is the first cousin of the slice, because both are born from the same out-to-in club-path.

Most pull hitters fall into the one-fix category, and incorporating a (-) element will solve the problem. In rare instances, the pull can be the problem of the two-fix golfer and is caused by swinging down into the ball on an out-to-in path to compensate for a backswing that is too wide/shallow (-). If not for swinging down violently to the left, the club would likely swing over the top of the ball and miss it completely.

For a one-fix golfer to neutralize a pull, I have some recommendations.

- **DURING THE DOWNSWING:** 1. Let your hips slide and shoulders tilt, keeping your head behind the ball; 2. Swing your arms and club more in-to-out.
- **DURING THE BACKSWING:** 1. Make a bigger shoulder and hip turn; 2. Flatten your arm and club swing.
- **IMPACT/FOLLOW-THROUGH:** 1. Swing your arms more in-to-out and right of the target line; 2. Restrict your shoulder and hip turn to the left.
- **AT ADDRESS:** 1. Tilt your spine more to the right and put more weight on your right leg; 2. Close your shoulders in relation to your hips.

If after incorporating a (-) swing element your pull suddenly becomes a (-) ball-flight miss, such as a shallow-top or a thin, then you're a two-fix golfer. The first thing you need to do is to neutralize the large (+) element in the second half of your swing. You know it's in the second half because your original ball-flight miss is always the same as the dominating element in the second half of the swing. You need to apply a (-) from the downswing or impact/follow-through charts.

When you do this, your ball flight will now be very shallow/wide (-), even to the point where you're hitting tops or thins, or maybe even a shallow whiff. I want you to keep practicing this new (-) element for at least a couple of sessions. Sometimes you can intuitively correct the second problem without having to incorporate another element. But if your ball-flight miss hasn't dramatically improved into a solid shot, then you will need to incorporate a (+) element from the address or backswing charts.

I have some recommendations.

- **DURING THE DOWNSWING:** 1. Swing your arms and club more in-to-out; 2. Thrust your right hip at the ball.
- **DURING IMPACT/FOLLOW-THROUGH:** 1. Swing more in-to-out and to the right of the target line; 2. Restrict your hip and shoulder turn to the left.

Now let's get rid of that (-) in the first half of your swing. Try any of these elements.

- **AT ADDRESS:** Bend your spine over more.
- **DURING THE BACKSWING:** 1. Point the shaft to the right of your target at the top (across the line); 2. Swing your arms and club more upright.

PULL CHECKLIST

BALL-FLIGHT MISS: (+)
FLIGHT DESCRIPTION: Left of your target with no curve.
IMPACT CONDITION: Divot pointing left of your target in direction of shot.

ONE-FIX GOLFER: Incorporate one (-) element from the prescribed order of downswing, backswing, impact/follow-through, address. Note: If your ball-flight miss doesn't improve, and instead changes to a (-), go to the instructions for the two-fix golfer.

RECOMMENDATIONS FOR THE ONE-FIX GOLFER: Down-swing: slide hips and tilt shoulders with head behind ball; or swing arms, club more in-to-out. Backswing: make a bigger shoulder, hip turn; or flatten arm, club swing. Impact/follow-through: swing arms, club more in-to-out and right of target line; or restrict shoulder, hip turn to the left. Address: tilt spine more to right and put more weight on right leg; close shoulders in relation to hips.

TWO-FIX GOLFER: After incorporating a (-) element from the downswing or impact/follow-through charts, practice it for a while. If your ball flight doesn't dramatically improve, incorporate a (+) element from the address or backswing charts.

RECOMMENDATIONS FOR THE TWO-FIX GOLFER: Fix No. 1—Downswing: swing arms and club more in-to-out; or thrust right hip at ball. Impact/follow-through: swing arms, club more in-to-out and to right of target line; or restrict hip, shoulder turn to left. Fix No. 2—Address: bend spine over more. Backswing: point shaft more to right at top; or swing arms, club more upright.

Chapter Six

FATS AND THINS, CHOPS AND CHUNKS

This chapter is near but not so dear to most golfers' hearts since, when learning the golf swing, almost everyone struggles to hit solid shots. Fats and thins and chops and chunks are misses in which the ball is not struck with the center of the clubface and the angle of approach is extremely exaggerated. Furthermore, it's almost always a weak hit. While fat and thin shots are always caused by the same swing elements, they most certainly are not produced the same way as chopped and chunked shots; in fact they are the opposite. Therefore, you must follow a different process to correct fat/thin shots than you would if your ball-flight miss was a chop/chunk.

Fat/thin shots are weak hits that almost always fly shorter than the distance the club is capable of producing. They are almost always caused by a clubpath that moves from inside the target line on the downswing to outside the target line on the follow-through. The path into the ball is so shallow/wide

(-) that the club either hits the ground before it reaches the ball (a fat) or reaches the low point before the ball and misses the ground completely, after which the leading edge of the club makes contact with the ball on the upswing and sends it off on a low trajectory (a thin). It should be noted that while the fat shot does not feel solid, a slightly thin shot can feel somewhat solid, since the ball is contacted cleanly. But regardless of the solidness of the hit, they're both (-) ball-flight misses.

Meanwhile, the chop/chunk is caused by a very steep/narrow (+) swing. It might seem like a fat shot, but the club's path typically moves from outside the target line on the downswing to inside the target line during the follow-through, which is the opposite path of the fat/thin. Because of the steepness of the approach into the impact zone, the club literally crashes into the turf. This is most definitely a (+) ball-flight miss. While the fat/thin could be a better player's problem—though not exclusively—the chop/chunk is almost always the ball-flight miss of a mid- to high-handicap player or a rank beginner.

Let's start with correcting the more common problem—the chop/chunk. The first thing you need to do is to identify the ball flight. If you're using a driver, the miss will typically be a pop-up, since the steepness of the path forces ball/club contact on top of the driver's face or, worse, on top of the clubhead. If the ball is on the ground, then the chop/chunk miss can be high or low in trajectory, but in either case it will not fly as far as the distance the club is capable of producing. The shot will not feel like it was solidly struck. As I said, this is a (+) ball-flight miss. The fat shot, which is a (-) ball-flight miss, can easily be mistaken for a chop/chunk, so it's important to verify which type of miss you're dealing with by looking at the ground where the ball used to be (impact condition).

The impact condition for a chop/chunk is usually a very deep divot that points left of your target. The divot can either start slightly behind the ball's position at address or right at the spot where it used to be. The good news is, if this is your predominant ball-flight miss, you can easily correct it by incorporating any one of dozens of new swing elements. In other words, you'll likely be a one-fix golfer and neutralize your current swing by adding one or more (-) elements. The (+) ball-flight and impact condition is always the result of having too many (+) elements in your swing. All you have to do is neutralize them to start hitting the ball more solidly. (Although I must add that in very rare circumstances, the (+) result at impact can be an overreaction to a backswing that is so shallow/wide (-) that the golfer has to swing violently down and to the left in order to have any chance at contact. That golfer is going to have to make two fixes to vanquish the chop/chunk.)

If you're in the one-fix category, you can choose any one (-) element from the four swing charts to correct this problem. Here are some of my recommendations that will help you neutralize your (+) ball flight. Remember to try them in the prescribed chart order (downswing, backswing, impact/follow-through, address).

- **DURING THE DOWNSWING:** 1. Thrust your right hip at the ball; 2. Restrict your shoulder turn.
- **DURING THE BACKSWING:** 1. Swing your arms and club flatter; 2. Make a bigger shoulder and hip turn.
- **DURING THE IMPACT/FOLLOW-THROUGH:** 1. Swing your arms and club more in-to-out and to the right of the target line; 2. Restrict your shoulder and hip turn to the left.
- **AT ADDRESS:** Stand farther away from the ball.

Any one of these elements could easily fix a chop/chunk. But there are lots and lots of choices you can try. You just have to find the one that's best for you. The reason I gave you some examples is that I've found they've worked the best for many of the students I've taught.

In the rare case that you aren't in the one-fix category and need two fixes to get rid of the chop/chunk, you'll know it because after incorporating a (-) element like the ones I just mentioned, your ball-flight miss will shift way past neutral and now be a (-) miss. The reason? You were hitting the chop/chunk as a compensation for an extremely shallow backswing. It was so shallow that you had to make an extremely steep out-to-in downswing in order to make contact with the ball.

Just like all two-fix golfers, what you need to do first is to identify the half of your swing where the major (+) element resides and neutralize it by incorporating a (-) element. In this case, you know the (+) is in the second half, because your ball flight is always the same as the large element in the second half. Since chops and chunks are a (+), that means the second half of the swing is too (+).

Now you need to neutralize that (+) element in the second half of your swing by incorporating a (-) element into your downswing or impact/follow-through. At this point, your ball flight will become very shallow/wide, even to the point where you're topping or whiffing above the ball. If this condition doesn't improve over time, and you learn intuitively to correct the too (-) compensation move you've been making in the first half of your swing, you'll need to incorporate a (+) element to either your address or backswing.

Here's the process I'd recommend.

- DURING THE DOWNSWING: 1. Slide your hips toward the target and tilt your shoulders, keeping your head behind the ball; 2. Swing your arms and club more in-to-out; 3. Thrust your right hip at the ball.
- DURING THE IMPACT/FOLLOW-THROUGH: 1. Keep some weight on the right leg, allowing the lower body to finish closer to the target than the upper body; 2. Swing your arms and club more in-to-out and to the right of the target.

Then, after you've practiced for a while to get used to the new fix in the second half of the swing, you're ready to neutralize the (-) in the first half of your swing. I have some recommendations.

- AT ADDRESS: Bend your spine over more.
- DURING THE BACKSWING: 1. Make a steeper shoulder turn; 2. Point the shaft more to the right at the top (across the line).

CHOP/CHUNK CHECKLIST

BALL-FLIGHT MISS: (+)

FLIGHT DESCRIPTION: Weak hit that flies shorter than the distance the club is capable of producing. Tee shots are often popped up.

IMPACT CONDITION: Deep divot starting at or behind the ball's position at address and likely pointing left of target.

CAUSE: Angle of attack is too steep and likely on an out-to-in path, causing the club to crash into the ground.

ONE-FIX GOLFER: Incorporate one (-) element from downswing, backswing, impact/follow-through, or address charts in this prescribed order. Note: If your ball-flight miss doesn't improve, and instead changes to a (-), go to the instructions for the two-fix golfer.

RECOMMENDATIONS FOR THE ONE-FIX GOLFER: Downswing: thrust right hip at ball; or restrict shoulder turn. Backswing: make flatter arm, club swing; or make bigger shoulder, hip turn. Impact/follow-through: swing arms, club more in-to-out and to the right of the target line; or restrict shoulder, hip turn. Address: stand farther from ball.

TWO-FIX GOLFER: If you've incorporated a (-) element from downswing or impact/follow-through charts and the ball flight doesn't dramatically improve after some practice, incorporate a (+) element from address or backswing charts.

RECOMMENDATIONS FOR THE TWO-FIX GOLFER: Fix No. 1—Downswing: slide hips and tilt shoulder with head behind ball; or swing arms, club more in-to-out; or thrust your right hip at the ball. Impact/follow-through: finish with upper body behind lower body, with some weight on right leg; or swing arms, club more in-to-out and to right of target. Fix No. 2—Address: bend spine over more. Backswing: make steeper shoulder turn; or point shaft more to right at top (across the line).

Now I'm going to show you how to deal with fat/thin shots. As I stated earlier, fats and thins are (-) ball flights. Just as with chop/chunk shots, most golfers will be able to make one adjustment to fix their current swing, rather than incorporate two fixes. Only in rare instances will two fixes be required. So let's get started. First, identify the ball-flight miss. The thing you'll notice about a fat shot is that it feels very weak when it comes off the club. The trajectory of a fat shot can vary, but it's typically a medium-lofted shot that flies shorter than you would expect. Sometimes, the club slides along the ground behind the ball and then bounces up into it, causing it to fly on a lower trajectory. But this is still a fat shot, since the club made contact with the ground before the ball. A thin, however, will probably feel a little more solid, because the leading edge of the club strikes the ball cleanly. The club either skims along the ground or never touches it at all and strikes the ball as the head is ascending. A thin shot is related to a fat shot, because they both approach the ball on an angle that is too shallow (-) for proper contact.

To verify that you hit a fat/thin shot, take a look at the ground where your ball used to be. The impact condition most noticeable with a fat shot is a shallow divot farther from the target than where the ball was at address. That divot will typically be pointing right of the target or at the target, but not left of the target. With a thin shot, however, there probably won't be any evidence of impact.

To fix a fat/thin ball-flight miss, you have to neutralize your shallow/wide (-) swing element. Here are some of my recommendations for (+) elements. Remember to try them in the prescribed order (downswing, backswing, impact/follow-through, address) of the charts.

- **DURING THE DOWNSWING:** 1. Move the entire body more toward the target and your weight onto your left leg; 2. Swing your arms and the club more to the left toward out-to-in.
- **DURING THE BACKSWING:** 1. Allow no head movement to the right while putting more weight on the left leg; 2. Swing your arms and club straighter back.
- **DURING THE IMPACT/FOLLOW-THROUGH:** 1. Shift your upper body directly over your lower body with all of your

weight on your left leg; 2. Lean the shaft forward; 3. Swing
your arms and club handle more to the left.

- AT ADDRESS: Lean the handle ahead of the ball.

Remember, my recommendations might not work for
you as well as some of the other elements in the charts do, so
feel free to try any element as long as it's a (+).

In rare instances, incorporating one (+) element might
shift your ball-flight miss from a (-) to a (+). If this happens
to you, you'll need two fixes to get rid of your fat/thin ball-
flight miss. Remember that as a two-fix golfer the reason
you're hitting fats and thins is that your swing has a
watermelon-size (+) element in the first half of your swing
and, to compensate for it, a watermelon-size (-) element in
the second half of your swing. One example of how this could
happen would be if you had a very steep backswing but
shifted your weight onto your back leg during the downswing
in an effort to hit the ball. This shift would cause an overly
shallow approach into the ball, and you would start to hit fats
and thins.

The first thing you should do is recognize that you have
a big (+) in the first half of your swing. And, like all two-fix
golfers, you have to neutralize the (+) before you deal with
the (-). In this case, the (+) occurs in the first half of your
swing, so you should apply a (-) element from either the address or backswing charts to neutralize the fact that you take
the club back so steeply.

After incorporating a (-), you'll probably be hitting very
shallow thins or even whiffing for a while. I want you to
keep practicing with this new element. Golfers sometimes
intuitively fix the compensation move without any further

adjustments. But if your ball-flight misses don't dramatically improve after a couple of sessions, you will now need to incorporate a (+) into the second half of your swing. Get one from either the downswing or impact/follow-through charts.

Here's what I'd recommend for the two-fix process.

- **AT ADDRESS:** Tilt your spine away from the target and put more weight on your right leg.
- **DURING THE BACKSWING:** 1. Make a bigger hip and shoulder turn; 2. Extend your arms wider, with less wrist cock and the club pointed more to the left at the top (laid off).

To neutralize the big (-) in the second half of your swing, here are my recommendations.

- **DURING THE DOWNSWING:** 1. Move your entire body toward the target and onto the left leg; 2. Swing your arms and club more to the left, toward out-to-in.
- **DURING IMPACT/FOLLOW-THROUGH:** 1. Make sure your upper body stays stacked over your lower body and all of your weight ends up on your left leg; 2. Lean the shaft forward; 3. Swing your arms and club handle more to the left.

FATS/THINS CHECKLIST

BALL-FLIGHT MISS: (-)
FLIGHT DESCRIPTION: Weak hit that flies shorter than the distance the club is capable of producing, but at various trajectories.

IMPACT CONDITIONS: A shallow divot behind the ball's position at address, usually pointing right of the target or at the target. There also may be no evidence of a divot.

CAUSE: The club is moving on an in-to-out path that's so shallow that the bottom of the swing occurs before the club reaches the ball. Sometimes the club never touches the ground.

ONE-FIX GOLFER: Incorporate one (+) element from the downswing, backswing, impact/follow-through, or address charts in this prescribed order. Note: If your ball-flight miss doesn't improve, and instead changes to a (+), go to the instructions for the two-fix golfer.

RECOMMENDATIONS FOR THE ONE-FIX GOLFER: Down-swing: move entire body toward target while shifting weight onto left leg; or swing arms, club more left, toward out-to-in. Backswing: no head movement to right and put more weight on left leg; or swing arms, club straighter back. Impact/follow-through: finish with upper body over lower body, weight on left leg; or lean shaft forward; or swing arms, club handle more to left. Address: lean handle ahead of ball.

TWO-FIX GOLFER: Incorporate a (-) element from the address or backswing charts. If after practicing your shots don't improve, then incorporate a (+) element from the downswing or impact/follow-through charts.

RECOMMENDATIONS FOR TWO-FIX GOLFER: Fix No. 1—Address: tilt spine to the right and put more weight on right leg. Backswing: make bigger hip and shoulder turn; or extend arms wider, with less wrist cock and the club pointed more to the left at the top (laid off).

Fix No. 2—Downswing: move entire body toward target,
putting weight onto the left leg; or swing arms, club more
to the left, toward out-to-in. Impact/follow-through: finish
with upper body stacked over lower body, all weight on left
leg; or lean shaft forward; or swing arms, club handle
more to the left.

Chapter Seven

HEEL/SHANK AND TOE HITS

There's nothing like the feeling of hitting the ball on the sweet spot and having it leap off the face. It feels effortless. But on the other end of the spectrum are off-center hits on the inner and outer edges of the clubface. They twist the clubhead, rotate the grip in your hands, and feel just plain awful. Hopefully you haven't had a lot of experience with these shots, but if you have, this chapter will explain how to start making center contact and experience the joys of hitting the ball in the middle of the club.

The outside edge of the clubface is referred to as the "toe," while the inside edge of the face (the part closest to the shaft) is the "heel." A ball hit with an iron excessively on the inside of the face, against the heel, is either a heel or a shank. Although they will produce different ball flights, these two shots are caused by the same problem. Conversely, a ball hit way out on the outer edge is—you guessed it—a toe hit. With the exception of missing the ball completely, these are perhaps the worst shots you can hit—especially because the ball flights are wild and completely unpredictable. Both high-handicappers and low-handicappers are capable of producing these ball-flight misses—even tour pros do it every now and then. Let me show you how heel and toe hits occur and walk you through how to correct them.

First let's correct the heel and shank, which are both in the (-) ball-flight miss category. Assuming you're not standing too close to the ball, the heel or shank is the result of a swing that's too shallow. It needs more narrow/steep (+) elements to match the distance you're standing away from the ball at address. What happens in a heel/shank is that your clubhead gets too far behind you during the backswing and then moves too far out in front of you during the downswing and impact, causing you to strike the ball on the heel of the clubface, instead of in its center. Although the ball flights produced by the heel and shank can vary, one thing's for sure when you're trying to identify whether you've hit one of these two shots— the ball won't fly nearly as far as the distance the club is capable of producing. The heel ball will likely have too much backspin and can balloon, particularly into the wind if you're using a driver or fairway wood off the tee. The ball also will likely fly right of your target. It slices with woods. But if you hit a shank with an iron, the ball flight will be straight right and lower than normal. Another telltale sign that you've hit one of these two shots? The club will probably reverberate in your hands.

As I said, these are both (-) ball-flight misses, so I'm grouping them together. To verify you've hit either one, check your clubface for ball marks. They should be clearly visible toward the heel—or even at the base of the shaft—of your club. If you're using a wood off the tee, check the sole of the club. The tee marks will be on the shaft side of the face closer to the heel. If the tee marks are slightly on the toe side of center, then your path is correct and this miss is not your issue.

The heel/shank is something you can usually overcome with only one fix to your swing. Since your swing is too shallow/wide, you need to incorporate a steep/narrow (+) element to start hitting it flush. I would strongly advise trying the specific (+) elements I'm about to recommend, and remember to try them in the order of charts prescribed here.

- **DURING THE DOWNSWING:** 1. Increase/lower your spine; 2. Close the clubface; 3. Swing your arms more left, toward out-to-in.
- **DURING THE BACKSWING:** 1. Swing your arms and club more upright; 2. Point the shaft right of your target at the top (across the line); 3. Make a steeper shoulder turn; 4. Restrict your hip turn; 5. Increase/lower your spine.
- **DURING THE IMPACT/FOLLOW-THROUGH:** 1. Close the clubface; 2. Swing your arms and club handle more to the left of your target.
- **AT ADDRESS:** Bend your spine over more.

Remember, you likely only need one of these recommendations to fix the heel/shank. It's up to you to pick the one that feels the best.

In rare cases, a heel/shank could fall into the two-fix category. How will you know if you need two fixes? If after incorporating a (+) element into your swing, as you would if you were a one-fix golfer, your shots don't dramatically improve and, instead, you're now hitting a ball-flight miss in the

(+) category (such as a chop/chunk or a pull), you'll need to go the two-fix route. The reason for this is that your (-) ball flight was the result of compensating for a huge (+) element in the first half of your swing. It's the classic case of having a large (+) element in the first half and trying to compensate for it with a large (-) element in the second half.

Just like all two-fix golfers, what you need to do is to first identify the half of your swing in which the major (+) element resides and neutralize it by incorporating a (-) element. In this case, you know the (+) is in the first half, because your ball flight is always the same as the large element in the second half. Since a heel/shank is a (-), that means the second half of the swing is too (-).

Now that you know the (+) is in the first half, neutralize it by incorporating a (-) from either the address or backswing charts. The recommended (-) elements are:

- **AT ADDRESS:** 1. Stand farther from the ball; 2. Tilt your spine more to the right with more weight on your right leg.
- **DURING THE BACKSWING:** 1. Make a bigger hip and shoulder turn; 2. Swing your arms and club more inside the target line; 3. Make a flatter shoulder turn.

Once you incorporate that (-), practice it for a while. If the heel/shank doesn't go away because of instinctive adjustments you make to get rid of the (-) in the second half of the swing, then incorporate a (+) from either the downswing or impact/follow-through charts to get rid of it. Try these:

- **DURING THE DOWNSWING:** 1. Increase/lower your spine; 2. Close the clubface; 3. Swing your arms more left, toward out-to-in.

- DURING THE IMPACT/FOLLOW-THROUGH: 1. Close the clubface; 2. Swing your arms and club handle more to the left of your target.

HEEL/SHANK CHECKLIST

BALL-FLIGHT MISS: (-)

FLIGHT DESCRIPTION: Travels shorter than the distance the club is capable of producing. With driver and fairway woods, will curve to the right and float in the air with too much backspin. With irons, the shank will likely fly straight right and lower than normal.

IMPACT CONDITION: Instead of looking at the ground, check the club. There will either be a ball mark close to the heel of the club or, if the ball was teed up, tee marks on the heel or shaft side of the middle part of the club's sole.

CAUSE: Swing is too flat.

ONE-FIX GOLFER: Incorporate one (+) element from the downswing, backswing, impact/follow-through, or address charts in this prescribed order. Note: If your ball-flight miss doesn't improve and instead changes to a (+), go to the instructions for the two-fix golfer.

RECOMMENDATIONS FOR THE ONE-FIX GOLFER: Downswing: lower spine; or close clubface; or swing arms more left, toward out-to-in. Backswing: swing club, arms more upright; or point shaft more right at the top (across the line); or steepen shoulder turn; or restrict hip turn; or lower spine angle. Impact/follow-through: close clubface; or swing arms, club handle more left. Address: bend spine over more.

TWO-FIX GOLFER: Incorporate a (-) element from either the address or backswing charts. If, after some practice, the

**heel/shank isn't corrected, incorporate a (+) from either
the downswing or impact/follow-through charts.
RECOMMENDATIONS FOR THE TWO-FIX GOLFER: Fix No.
1—Address: stand farther from ball; or tilt spine to the
right with more weight on right leg. Backswing: turn hips,
shoulders more; or swing more inside with arms, club; or
turn shoulders flatter. Fix No. 2—Downswing: increase/
lower spine; or close clubface; or swing arms more left,
toward out-to-in. Impact/follow-through: close clubface; or
swing arms, club handle more left of target.**

Now, let's correct toe hits. Assuming you're not standing
too far from the ball, the toe is a (+) ball-flight miss. It's most
often the result of a swing that has too many (+) elements to
allow you to hit the ball on the center of the clubface. Simply
put, your swing is too upright and the club does not swing far
enough behind you in the backswing and therefore does not
swing far enough out in front of you in the downswing to meet
the ball in the right spot. Instead, you contact the ball with the
toe. In extreme cases, the ball can be nicked off the very outside of the clubhead, resulting in a rare toe-shank, and the ball
will shoot off to the right, nearly perpendicular to your target.

One telltale sign that you're suffering from toe hits is that
the ball doesn't come close to flying the distance it should
have flown with the club you're using (and most likely didn't
fly anywhere near where you intended it to go). The reason is
that a severe toe hit can't produce enough backspin to keep
the ball airborne for a significant length of time, and the
glancing blow often shoots the ball nowhere near your intended target. If you hit a toe shot with an iron, it might
sound and feel like you've broken the club. Another sign that
you're hitting shots out on the toe is if you hit a hook (Chap-

ter Five) with your driver or fairway woods, or hit the ball slightly wayward to the right with your irons.

To verify you're hitting toe shots, instead of checking the ground like you do for most ball-flight misses, you should check your clubface. What you're most likely going to see is a ball mark way out on the outer edge of the clubhead. Or, if you've just hit a tee shot with a driver or a fairway wood, look at the bottom of the club and see if the tee marks on the sole of the club are excessively close to the toe. By that, I mean that on a correct center hit, the tee marks will be slightly on the toe side of center because of the club's in-to-in path. But if your tee marks are farther out on the toe side of the sole, you've likely produced a toe hit.

Almost all golfers who hit toe shots can correct the problem with one fix. Since it's a (+) ball-flight miss, all you need to do is incorporate a (-) element to make your swing less steep/narrow. While most ball-flight misses allow you to choose from dozens of elements to correct the problem, the toe is special. In my experience, the following (-) elements will work the best.

- **DURING THE DOWNSWING:** 1. Swing your arms and club more in-to-out; 2. Thrust your right hip at the ball.
- **DURING THE BACKSWING:** 1. Make a flatter swing with your arms and club; 2. Extend your arms wider, with less wrist cock and get the shaft pointed more left at the top; 3. Make a flatter shoulder turn; 4. Make a bigger hip and shoulder turn.
- **DURING THE IMPACT/FOLLOW-THROUGH:** Swing your arms and club more in-to-out and to the right of your target line.
- **AT ADDRESS:** Stand with your spine more upright.

Any one of these elements will do the trick. It's up to you to choose the one that feels and works the best for you.

In very rare cases, the toe ball-flight miss requires two fixes. If this is you, it means you have a big (-) element in the first half of your swing and you're trying to compensate for it with a big (+) element in the second half of your swing. The compensation move is the reason why you're producing toe hits, but in reality, your swing is too (-). You'll know you fall into the two-fix category if, after incorporating a (-) into your swing like all the one-fix golfers, your toe ball flight suddenly turns into a (-) ball flight, such as a fat, thin, or shallow-top.

Just like all two-fix golfers, what you need to do is to first identify the half of your swing where the major (+) element resides and neutralize it by incorporating a (-) element. In this case, you know the (+) is in the second half, because your ball-flight miss is always the same as the large element in the second half. Since a toe hit is a (+), that means the second half of the swing is too (+).

To neutralize the (+), I recommend the following:

- **DURING THE DOWNSWING:** 1. Swing your arms and club more in-to-out; 2. Thrust your right hip at the ball.
- **DURING THE IMPACT/FOLLOW-THROUGH:** Swing your arms and club more in-to-out and to the right of your target line.

Practice this element for some time, even though you will probably hit a lot of (-) ball-flight misses. Your shots might eventually improve and get back to neutral. If the problem doesn't go away naturally, you'll have to incorporate a (+) in the first half of your swing to deal with the big (-) element located at the top of your backswing. I have some recommendations.

- AT ADDRESS: 1. Stand closer to the ball; 2. Bend your spine over more.
- DURING THE BACKSWING: 1. Restrict your hip turn; 2. Steepen your shoulder turn.

TOE HIT CHECKLIST

BALL-FLIGHT MISS: (+)

FLIGHT DESCRIPTION: Travels shorter than the distance the club is capable of producing. Falls out of the sky due to lack of backspin. Direction of ball is unpredictable but often to the right of target with irons and curving to the left with a driver or fairway wood.

IMPACT CONDITION: Instead of looking at the ground, check the club. There will either be a ball mark out toward the toe of the club, or if the ball was teed up, evidence of tee marks out toward the toe on the bottom of the club.

CAUSE: The swing is too upright.

ONE-FIX GOLFER: Incorporate one (-) element from the downswing, backswing, impact/follow-through, or address charts in this prescribed order. Note: If your ball-flight miss doesn't improve, and instead changes to a (-), go to the instructions for the two-fix golfer.

RECOMMENDATIONS FOR THE ONE-FIX GOLFER: Down-swing: swing arms more in-to-out; or thrust right hip at ball. Backswing: swing arms, club flatter, with less wrist cock and shaft pointing left at top; or make a flatter shoulder turn; or make a bigger hip, shoulder turn. Impact/follow-through: swing arms, club more in-to-out and to right of target line. Address: stand with spine more upright.

TWO-FIX GOLFER: Incorporate a (-) from either the downswing or impact/follow-through charts. If ball flight doesn't dramatically improve after some practice, incorporate a (+) from either the address or backswing charts.

RECOMMENDATIONS FOR THE TWO-FIX GOLFER: Fix No. 1—Address: stand closer to ball; or bend spine over more. Backswing: restrict hip turn; or make a steeper shoulder turn. Fix No. 2— Downswing: swing arms, club more in-to-out; or thrust right hip at ball. Impact/follow-through: swing arms, club more in-to-out and to right of target line.

Chapter Eight

SHOTS THAT DON'T GET OFF THE GROUND

The topped shot is one of the most frustrating in golf, but not all tops are created equal. There are two ways to produce this ball-flight miss, but before I explain the differences, let me first describe what a top looks like. If your club makes contact with the ball at or above its equator, then it's impossible to get your shot off the ground. The ball will just bound along the turf. That's why the shot is called a "top"—your club has hit the top half of the ball. You can top a shot either with a steep approach into the ball—a (+) ball-flight miss—or you can top it with an approach that's so shallow that you actually hit the ball above its equator as your club is level to the ground or ascending. That's a (-) ball-flight miss. No matter which of these misses you have, your swing is way out of balance. It's either a case of too many pluses or too many minuses. I'll walk you through the process to correct either situation.

First, let's deal with the miss I call the "shallow-top." You'll get your first clue that you've hit this shot if the ball is running along the ground—most often skipping across the turf. It's almost always produced with a fairway wood or a long iron, rarely with a mid iron, and almost never with a short iron, although it can be hit with short shots around the green. To verify that you've hit the shallow-top, check the ground where the ball was at address. Typically with this shot, there will either be no evidence of a divot or a shallow divot well behind the ball's position at address. As I mentioned earlier, this shot is produced by swinging into the ball on an extremely shallow angle. Remember my airport analogies from the early chapters? The plane is approaching the runway on such a shallow angle that it's either circling the field or making touchdown short of the runway. If it does land short, it barely skims the ground before the runway. Otherwise it just keeps circling and never lands at all. In other words, your club either makes contact with the top half of the ball—without touching the ground—or it skims the ground well behind the ball and then makes contact on the upswing. Golfers most often hit this shot as a result of trying to help the ball into the air by swinging up on it. This is a severely shallow (-) ball-flight miss.

If you're hitting a shallow-top, you can only be in the one-fix golfer category. Golfers who hit the steep-top are in the two-fix category. We'll deal with that problem later in this chapter. Back to shallow-toppers. If this is you, what you have to do is incorporate as many (+) elements as it takes to start getting the ball airborne. One element probably won't do the trick. Your impact is so severely (-) that you'll likely have to incorporate more than one (+) element to correct the problem. Think of it as adding more and more weight to one side of a scale until it balances out. If the first (+) element doesn't balance the scale, either exaggerate it or incorporate another—and possibly even another—until you get the desired result. You can choose from any of the (+) elements in the charts, but here are my recommendations, based on success I've had helping others overcome this problem. Remember, incorporate only one element at a time to see how much it helps correct the top. If it doesn't help much, then incorporate something else and keep incorporating things until your shots dramatically improve. And remember to try these elements in the chart order that I prescribe here:

- **DURING THE DOWNSWING:** 1. Move your entire body more toward the target and onto your left leg; 2. Lower your spine.
- **DURING THE BACKSWING:** 1. Swing your arms and club on a more upright plane; 2. Make a steeper shoulder turn.
- **DURING THE IMPACT/FOLLOW-THROUGH:** 1. Swing more down into the ball; 2. Lean the shaft more forward; 3. Get your upper body to finish directly over your lower body, with all of your weight on your left foot.
- **AT ADDRESS:** Bend your spine over more and stand closer to the ball.

Now, when you incorporate a (+) element into your swing, you may suddenly experience a (+) ball flight, such as a chop/chunk, instead of hitting the shallow-top or getting your swing back to neutral. What has happened is that your miss is actually a steep-top rather than a shallow-top. The steep-top is the problem of a two-fix golfer, and you should immediately go to the section in this chapter that deals with the steep-top.

SHALLOW-TOP CHECKLIST

BALL-FLIGHT MISS: (-)

FLIGHT DESCRIPTION: Runs along the ground, often in a skipping motion.

IMPACT CONDITION: No evidence of a divot, or a very shallow divot well behind the ball's location at address.

CAUSE: The clubhead has bottomed out behind the ball and is ascending when it contacts the ball. Or, the clubhead is moving on a shallow path just above the ground and it clips the top of the ball. It's usually a product of an exaggerated in-to-out path at impact or an overly flat swing. It can also be caused by falling back onto the rear foot during the downswing or the impact/follow-through.

ONE-FIX GOLFER: Incorporate as many (+) elements as necessary from the downswing, backswing, impact/follow-through, or address charts, in this prescribed order. Note: If your ball-flight miss changes to a (+) after incorporating one or more pluses, you have misdiagnosed your original ball-flight miss. You are hitting a steep-top (+). Go to the instructions for the steep-top.

RECOMMENDATIONS FOR THE ONE-FIX GOLFER: Downswing: move entire body, head, hips more toward target and onto left leg; or increase/lower spine. Backswing: swing arms, club on more upright plane; or make steeper shoulder turn. Impact/follow-through: swing more down into the ball; or increase forward lean of shaft; or get your

upper body to finish directly over your lower body with all
of your weight on your left foot. Address: stand closer to
the ball and bend your spine over more.

Now let's deal with the steep-top. Again, you'll recognize
you're topping the ball when it runs along the ground. But
with this shot, you might also see that it takes big hops as it
bounds down the fairway. Unlike a shallow-top, the steep-top
can be produced with any iron, hybrid, or wood—even a
wedge. As I mentioned earlier, this ball-flight miss is produced by taking a very steep angle of approach into the ball
but then swinging up at the last second to avoid crashing the
club into the ground. The rapid upswing causes the club to
hit the top half of the ball.

Even though you're swinging up on the ball at impact,
this is a severely (+) ball-flight miss, because the very (-) element that causes the top is the result of the very steep position
at the top of the backswing. Think of a plane taking too steep
an approach into a runway and then having to pull up at the
last second to avoid crashing. When checking impact conditions, you will often find a very deep divot and some chop/
chunk shots (Chapter Six) accompanying this miss. But there
might not be any evidence of a divot at all. If the ball was on
a tee, it's also common to pop the shot up and break the tee.

The upswing portion of this miss is an attempt to compensate for being too steep into the ball. Therefore, you'll
need two fixes to get rid of this problem. It's possible that you
could be in a great position at the top of the swing but still hit
the steep-top. I've seen instances in which a golfer has a very
steep downswing followed by a quick upswing at impact, but
it's very rare. No matter how it's caused, though, it will take
two fixes to neutralize.

Let's start by dealing with the steep (+) swing elements. Remember, whenever you fall into the two-fix category, the first thing you have to do is locate and neutralize the half of the swing where the overly (+) elements reside. In this case, they're in the first half of your swing. You know this because the ball-flight miss is always the same as the dominant element in the second half of the swing. In this case, they are both (-).

Not only do you need to start by dealing with the (+) in the first half of the swing, things could be so severely (+) that you might have to incorporate more than one (-) element to balance things out. You can incorporate (-) elements from either the address or the backswing chart. How many minuses will you have to incorporate? Think of adding weights to one side of a scale. One might do it, but if not, keep piling on more until the scale balances. Once all those pluses are neutralized, you can then deal with your compensation move of swinging up on the ball. This is a (-) condition, so you'll need to incorporate one (+) element to your downswing or impact/follow-through segment before you can get rid of the steep-top.

For the first step of neutralizing the way-too-steep pluses in the first half of your swing, you can choose from any number of (-) elements. But you might want to try my recommendations:

- **AT ADDRESS:** Tilt your spine more to the right and put more weight onto your right leg.
- **DURING THE BACKSWING:** 1. Make a bigger hip and shoulder turn; 2. Flatten your arm and club swing; 3. Extend your arms wider and cock your wrists less.

Now that you've incorporated the appropriate amount of minuses to take care of those severely steep swing elements, you'll probably be really topping badly or even whiffing. Practice with only the minus elements that you've incorporated into your address or backswing for a little while, to see if the top doesn't go away naturally—now that you've eliminated the reason you had to suddenly pull up, it just might. If it doesn't go away, you need a (+) element to correct your compensation move of swinging up on the ball during the second half of your swing.

Here are my recommendations.

- **DURING THE DOWNSWING:** 1. Shift all of your body weight onto your left leg; 2. Lower your spine angle.
- **DURING IMPACT/FOLLOW-THROUGH:** 1. Swing more down at the ball; 2. Finish with your upper body directly over your lower body and have all of your weight supported by your left leg.

STEEP-TOP CHECKLIST

BALL-FLIGHT MISS: (+)

FLIGHT DESCRIPTION: Runs along the ground, often taking big hops.

IMPACT CONDITION: No evidence of a divot or, on occasion, a very deep divot behind the ball's location at address.

CAUSE: A very steep first half of the swing (+), followed by the compensation move of an abrupt upswing (-) near impact to avoid crashing the club into the turf.

ONE-FIX GOLFER: N/A

RECOMMENDATIONS FOR THE ONE-FIX GOLFER: N/A

TWO-FIX GOLFER: Incorporate as many (-) elements as necessary from the address or backswing charts. Then, if your swing hasn't improved after a period of practice,

incorporate a (+) element from the downswing or impact/
follow-through charts.

RECOMMENDATIONS FOR THE TWO-FIX GOLFER: Fix No.
1—Address: tilt spine to right, put more weight on right
leg. Backswing: turn hips, shoulders more; or swing arms,
club flatter; or swing arms wider, hinge wrists less. Fix
No. 2—Downswing: shift entire body weight onto left leg;
or increase/lower spine. Impact/follow-through: swing
more down on the ball; or finish with upper body directly
over the lower body, 100 percent of weight on left leg; or
lean shaft forward.

Chapter Nine

SHOTS THAT FLY TOO LOW

You might know it as the worm-burner, the screamer, or the headhunter, but there's more than one way to mishit a shot and produce an unintentionally low trajectory. One such way is to come down into the ball on a very steep path and literally trap it against the turf with the face of the club. Since the club is in a delofted and usually closed position, it often produces a line drive. I call this the "steep-trap." This is a (+) ball-flight miss and a common problem of high-handicap players and rank beginners. The other flat-trajectory shot is the "low-shallow," which is very similar to the "thin" shot discussed in Chapter Six. This shot is more likely produced when the ball is on the ground and the golfer is using a lower-lofted club. But it also can be produced with just about any club. You might refer to this as a "skulled" shot if you're using a wedge. The low-shallow, just like it sounds, is a product of a very shallow approach into the ball, which forces contact toward the bottom of the clubface. Just like the thin, this is a (-) ball-flight miss and is a problem for both high- and low-handicappers. But no matter which low-trajectory miss you might struggle with, your shot will typically go straight or will miss to the left of your target. In really severe cases, these shots won't even get off the ground and are shallow- or steep-tops, which are discussed in Chapter Eight.

Let's deal with the "steep-trap" first. Identifying this ball flight should be fairly simple. As I said, the ball is usually going to fly low and left if it gets airborne. You can hit this shot with just about any club in the bag, with perhaps the exception of your short irons and wedges.

To confirm this ball-flight miss, you should take a look at the ground where your ball was sitting at address. The impact condition you'll likely find is a deep divot pointing to the left of your target. The reason for the deep crater is that the steep/narrow (+) path, combined with a delofted and shut face, turns your club into a digging tool. The divot often points to the left of your target because it matches the direction of your clubpath, which comes from outside your target line on the downswing to inside your target line during the follow-through. In addition to the low ball flight and deep divot, contact will not be solid and sometimes occur high on the clubface.

In almost all cases, you can vanquish the steep-trap by making one fix instead of two. But even a one-fix golfer might also have to do a second fix to adjust the clubface to optimize the impact and resulting ball flight. Sometimes this shot is the result of having the double (+) situation of a steep downswing and closed clubface. Therefore, even though one fix might get the job done for many, some of you will have to incorporate two (-) elements into your swing. But first, shallow out your impact. That will tell you if you need to incorporate another (-).

In my experience, certain elements work better than others to get the job done, so I'll give you some recommendations. However, you should feel free to try any of the elements from the (-) side of the charts until something clicks for you. Remember to try them from the chart order prescribed here.

- DURING THE DOWNSWING: 1. Thrust your right hip at the ball while restricting your shoulder turn; 2. Swing your arms and club more in-to-out.
- DURING THE BACKSWING: 1. Extend your arms wider, with less wrist cock and point the club to the left at the top (laid off); 2. Make a bigger hip and shoulder turn; 3. Make a flatter arm and club swing.
- DURING THE IMPACT/FOLLOW-THROUGH: 1. Keep the handle of the clubshaft even with or slightly behind the clubhead's position at impact; 2. Swing your arms and club more in-to-out and to the right of your target; 3. Swing more up at the ball.
- AT ADDRESS: 1. Set the handle of your clubshaft so that it's even with the clubhead and pointing straight up and down; 2. Close your shoulders in relation to your hips.

If your ball flight is still too low after you've incorporated a (-) element to shallow out your approach, you'll have to incorporate another (-) to deal with that double (+) situation I mentioned earlier. Incorporate another element only if your impact didn't improve dramatically after incorporating the first (-) element. I recommend any of the following to correct the problem:

- AT ADDRESS: Weaken your grip.
- DURING THE DOWNSWING: Open the clubface.

- **DURING THE IMPACT/FOLLOW-THROUGH:** Open or
  block with the clubface.

Any one of these (-) elements, coupled with the earlier adjustment, should get you hitting shots higher and more solidly.

Now let's deal with the two-fix golfer who is hitting steep-traps. How will you know if you're a two-fix candidate? If you incorporate a (-) into your swing and your ball-flight miss then goes from a steep-trap to a (-) ball-flight miss, you're going to require two fixes instead of one. You were hitting the steep-trap as a compensation for an extremely shallow backswing. It was so shallow that you had to make an extremely steep out-to-in downswing in order to make contact with the ball.

To remedy this situation, first incorporate a (-) into your (+) downswing. Whenever you fall into the two-fix category, you always want to deal with the half of your swing where the (+) element dominates. In this case, it's the second half of the swing. You'll know that because the original ball-flight miss and the elements in the second half of the swing are always the same. In this case, pluses.

After you incorporate a (-) from either the downswing or impact/follow-through chart, you might start hitting shots that are more solid, but hooking. Now you will need to make a clubface alteration to vanquish this (-) ball-flight miss. After making that second adjustment, keep practicing to see if your shots eventually improve and the problem goes away. Sometimes you will intuitively make adjustments without further help. If your shots don't improve and you start hitting thins or shallow-tops as a result of incorporating a (-) in the second half of the swing, you now need to incorporate a (+) from either the address or backswing chart to neutralize the problem.

If you're doing the math, you're probably aware that

many of you will have to make three adjustments, instead of two, to banish the steep-trap. I know that might sound confusing—just like how some one-fix golfers have to do two things to neutralize the steep-trap. But trust me, this is the only way some of you can get back to neutral. So here's the process I'd recommend.

- **DURING THE DOWNSWING:** 1. Thrust your right hip at the ball while restricting your shoulder turn; 2. Swing your arms and club more in-to-out.
- **DURING THE IMPACT/FOLLOW-THROUGH:** 1. Swing your arms and club more in-to-out and right of your target line; 2. Restrict your shoulder and hip turn; 3. Swing more up at the ball.

Now you might be hitting a hook/slap-left, a low-shallow, or some other (-) ball-flight miss. If your miss is a hook/slap-left, you might need to make three adjustments instead of two. You have a closed clubface that we'll have to deal with, but not just yet. First you need to neutralize the overly (-) first half of your swing. To do that, you only need to make either your address or backswing more (+). One of these elements should do the trick.

- **AT ADDRESS:** Bend your spine over more.
- **DURING THE BACKSWING:** 1. Make a steeper shoulder turn; 2. Put more weight on your left leg with no head movement to the right; 3. Point the shaft more to the right of your target at the top (across the line).

At this point, if you're hooking shots, you need to make that third fix.

- AT ADDRESS: Weaken your grip. (If you're not hooking, then there's no need for you to make that third adjustment.)

This process is a little more complicated than correcting other ball-flight errors, so let's review one more time. You first need to incorporate a (-) from either the downswing or impact/follow-through chart. Again, my recommendations aren't the only choices you should try. Feel free to experiment with any element that might feel better or be easier to incorporate. Once you've done that, now incorporate a (+) swing element into either your address or backswing. If you're hooking after both those processes, weaken your grip at address.

STEEP-TRAP CHECKLIST

BALL-FLIGHT MISS: (+)

FLIGHT DESCRIPTION: Low trajectory or doesn't get off the ground when using lower-lofted clubs. Usually goes left of your target and can be produced with any club except the short irons and wedges.

IMPACT CONDITION: Deep divot pointing left of target.

CAUSE: Angle of attack is too steep and club is delofted (and sometimes closed).

ONE-FIX GOLFER: Incorporate one (-) element from downswing, backswing, impact/follow-through, or address charts in this prescribed order. If shot trajectory doesn't improve, incorporate a specific (-) element from the address, downswing, or impact/follow-through charts to adjust the clubface position at impact. Note: If you suddenly start hitting (-) ball flights after incorporating one or both of these fixes, go to the instructions for the two-fix golfer.

RECOMMENDATIONS FOR THE ONE-FIX GOLFER: Downswing: thrust right hip at ball; or restrict shoulder turn; or swing arms, club more in-to-out. Backswing: extend arms wider, cock wrists less, point club left at top; or make a bigger hip, shoulder turn; or make a flatter arm, club swing. Impact/follow-through: keep shaft even or behind clubhead; or swing arms, club more in-to-out and to right of target; or swing more up at the ball. Address: set handle/shaft pointing straight up and down; or close shoulders in relation to hips. Note: If flight is still too low and left, incorporate one of these (-) elements. Address: weaken grip. Downswing: open clubface. Impact/follow-through: open or block with clubface.

TWO-FIX GOLFER: Incorporate a (-) element from either downswing or impact/follow-through chart. Then, if ball flight doesn't improve after some practice, incorporate a (+) from the address or backswing charts. If you're hooking shots, incorporate a third, specific element from the address chart (weaken your grip).

RECOMMENDATIONS FOR THE TWO-FIX GOLFER: Fix No. 1—Downswing: thrust right hip at ball while restricting shoulder turn; or swing arms, club more in-to-out. Impact/follow-through: swing arms, club more in-to-out and right of target line; or swing more up at ball; or restrict shoulder, hip turn. Fix No. 2—Address: bend spine over more. Backswing, put more weight on left leg with no head movement to right; or make steeper shoulder turn or point the shaft to the right at top (across the line). Note: If impact is more solid, but the ball is hooking, make the following clubface adjustment—address: weaken grip.

To identify a low-shallow ball-flight miss, you'll notice that this problem occurs mostly with your longer irons and low-lofted fairway woods off of tight lies. This hit won't feel solid, and the ball typically won't travel as far as the distance the club is capable of producing. The reason this happens is that you're coming in to the ball on too shallow an angle of approach. Without a steep enough angle of attack to hit down, under, and then back up, the ball can't slide up the face of the lower-lofted clubs enough to achieve the proper launch angle. To verify that you're hitting low-shallows, check the impact conditions. What you'll typically find is no evidence of a divot, or a very shallow divot starting behind the ball's position at address. In other words, the club's approach to the ball was so shallow that it either barely skimmed the ground behind the ball before striking it or never touched the ground at all.

The low-shallow ball-flight miss is sometimes corrected with one fix, but in other cases, two fixes will be required. Remember, the fault causing this ball-flight miss is a shallow/wide impact (-). If your swing is in the one-fix category, then simply incorporating a (+) element will neutralize the problem and your shots will improve. Sometimes, however, the shallow/wide impact (-) is an overreaction to a swing that has too many (+) elements. I'll walk you through this process to see whether you can simply make one fix or will have to make two.

To fix a low-shallow miss, I'd recommend incorporating one of these (+) elements (remember to incorporate them from the specific order I give here).

- **DURING THE DOWNSWING:** 1. Shift your body weight onto your left leg; 2. Swing your arms and club more left, toward an out-to-in path.

- DURING THE BACKSWING: 1. Make a steeper shoulder turn; 2. Increase your spine angle by lowering it; 3. Make a more upright arm and club swing.
- DURING THE IMPACT/FOLLOW-THROUGH: 1. Swing more down at the ball; 2. Make a bigger shoulder and hip turn around to the left.
- AT ADDRESS: Bend your spine over more.

If you incorporate one of these (+) elements and you start to hit even worse shots—steep-tops or chop-chunks—then you know you're in the two-fix camp. Why did things get worse? As a two-fix golfer, you have two watermelon-size elements working against each other. Even though you have a low-shallow (-) ball flight, the first half of your swing is too steep/narrow (+) and you compensate with a second half of the swing that's too (-).

What you need to do is first deal with the huge (+) element located in the first half of your swing. Whenever you fall into the two-fix category, you always want to deal with the half of your swing where the (+) element dominates. In this case, it's the first half. You will know that because the original ball-flight miss and the elements in the second half of the swing are always the same. In this case, they were both minuses.

So you'll need to first incorporate a (-) element from the address or backswing charts to neutralize the problem in the first half of your swing. You've got a lot of elements to choose from, but I'd recommend the following.

- AT ADDRESS: Tilt your spine more to the right and put more weight on your right leg.
- DURING THE BACKSWING: 1. Make a flatter shoulder

turn; 2. Make a flatter arm and club swing; 3. Make a
bigger shoulder and hip turn.

Any one of these choices will neutralize the overly (+)
nature of the first half of your swing.

Unfortunately, after taking that step successfully, you'll
now be hitting some tops and even whiffing. But keep practicing. Sometimes you'll instinctively make adjustments to
get rid of the compensation move you've been making, and
you won't have to make any more adjustments to start hitting
good shots. But if that doesn't happen in a short time, incorporate a (+) element in the second half of your swing to neutralize the (-) compensation you've been making.

Here are my suggestions:

- DURING THE DOWNSWING: 1. Move your entire body
  toward the target and onto your left leg; 2. Close the
  clubface.
- DURING THE IMPACT/FOLLOW-THROUGH: 1. Get your
  upper body to finish directly over your lower body with all
  your weight on your left leg; 2. Lean the shaft forward and
  hit down on the ball more.

Again, these recommendations might not work for you
as well as other elements in the charts, so feel free to experiment until you find the right adjustments.

LOW-SHALLOW CHECKLIST

BALL-FLIGHT MISS: (-)
FLIGHT DESCRIPTION: Low trajectory and travels shorter
than the distance the club is capable of delivering. Typically

produced with less-lofted fairway woods and longer irons off the ground, but can be "skulled" short irons and wedges.

IMPACT CONDITION: Very shallow divot behind ball's position at address, or no evidence of a divot.

CAUSE: Shallow angle of attack forces the bottom of the club to hit the ball on the upswing.

ONE-FIX GOLFER: Incorporate one (+) element from the downswing, backswing, impact/follow-through, or address charts in this prescribed order. Note: If your ball-flight miss doesn't improve, and instead changes to a (+), go to the instructions for the two-fix golfer.

RECOMMENDATIONS FOR THE ONE-FIX GOLFER: Downswing: shift weight onto left leg; or swing arms, club more left, toward out-to-in. Backswing: steepen shoulder turn; or increase/lower spine; or swing arms, club more upright. Impact/follow-through: swing more down on ball; or make bigger shoulder, hip turn to left. Address: bend spine over more.

TWO-FIX GOLFER: Incorporate a (-) from the address or backswing charts. Then, if your shots and ball flight don't dramatically improve after some practice, incorporate a (+) from the downswing or impact/follow-through charts.

RECOMMENDATIONS FOR THE TWO-FIX GOLFER: Fix No. 1—Address: tilt spine more to right and put more weight on right leg. Backswing: turn shoulders flatter; swing arms, club flatter. Fix No. 2—Downswing: shift entire body toward target onto left leg; or close clubface. Impact/follow-through: finish with upper body over lower body with all weight on left leg; or lean shaft forward; or hit more down at ball.

Chapter Ten

SHOTS THAT FLY TOO HIGH

There are two ways to hit a ball too high in the air, and the method to correct them has been covered in earlier chapters, because they are produced the same way as other ball-flight misses. But rather than have you refer to earlier chapters to get rid of these problems, let's briefly review them here.

There's the "high-shallow," which I will talk about later in this chapter, and then there's the "high-steep." The high-steep is a (+) ball-flight miss and is produced when the golf club swings down, under, and then up on the ball, launching it nearly straight up in the air. When hit with an iron, it will leave a deep divot. And when a driver or fairway wood passes under a teed-up ball, the result is a pop-up that goes a much shorter distance than normal. The high-steep is really exaggerated into the wind because the steep impact causes excessive backspin, making the ball "upshoot" and go very short distances. The error that produces this miss is the same as the swing fault that causes the chop/chunk in Chapter Six.

If you're hitting these shots, it's because you have a very

steep/narrow (+) swing. It should be easy enough to tell that you've hit this shot, because of your ball flight, but you can also verify it by your impact condition. If you used a wooden tee, it will probably be snapped in half and—even though you teed up the shot—there could also be a divot. When you hit this shot with an iron, you should expect to see a very deep divot.

The (+) ball flight and impact condition are always the result of having too many (+) elements in your swing. All you have to do is neutralize the (+) to start hitting your tee shots lower and more solidly. (Although I must add that in very rare circumstances, the (+) result at impact can be an over-reaction to a backswing that is so shallow/wide (-) that the golfer has to swing violently down and to the left in order to have any chance at contact. In that case, the golfer is going to have to make two fixes to get rid of the high-steep.)

If you're in the one-fix category, here are some of my recommendations for (-) elements that you can incorporate into your swing to neutralize your (+) ball flight.

- **DURING THE DOWNSWING:** 1. Thrust your right hip at the ball; 2. Restrict your shoulder turn.
- **DURING THE BACKSWING:** 1. Swing your arms and club flatter; 2. Make a bigger shoulder and hip turn.
- **DURING THE IMPACT/FOLLOW-THROUGH:** 1. Swing your arms and club more in-to-out and to the right of your target line; 2. Restrict your shoulder and hip turn to the left; 3. Swing more up at the ball.
- **AT ADDRESS:** Stand farther away from the ball.

Any one of these elements should easily fix the high-steep ball flight. But as I said in earlier chapters, there are lots and lots of choices you can try.

If, after incorporating a (-) element, you start hitting a (-) ball-flight miss, such as a top or a thin shot, then you're a two-fix golfer. As with all two-fix golfers, what you need to do is to first identify the half of your swing where the major (+) element resides and neutralize it by incorporating a (-) element. In this case, you know the (+) is in the second half, because your ball flight is always the same as the large element in the second half. Since a high-steep is a (+), that means the second half of the swing is too (+).

You'll first need to incorporate a (-) element from the downswing or impact/follow-through charts. That, unfortunately, will probably make your swing so shallow that you might even whiff. But if you don't intuitively correct the problem in the first half of your swing after some practice with the fix in the second half of your swing, you'll need to incorporate a (+) element into either the address or backswing to neutralize the big (-) element that's causing you to compensate in the second half and produce the high-steep. Here's the process and some of the elements I'd recommend.

- **DURING THE DOWNSWING:** 1. Let your hips slide toward the target and your upper body tilt away from it; 2. Thrust your right hip at the ball while restricting your shoulder turn.
- **DURING THE IMPACT/FOLLOW-THROUGH:** 1. Keep some weight on your right leg and allow the lower body to finish closer to the target than the upper body; 2. Swing more up at the ball.

Now, assuming that you didn't naturally correct the issue in the first half of your swing, you need to neutralize the (-) element. Some suggestions:

- AT ADDRESS: Bend your spine over more.
- DURING THE BACKSWING: 1. Make a steeper shoulder turn; 2. Point the shaft more to the right at the top (across the line).

Remember, you can choose any elements if these don't work for you. And if you follow the succession of first getting rid of the (+) in the second half of your swing, and then getting rid of the (-) in the first half, you should no longer be hitting a high-steep shot.

HIGH-STEEP CHECKLIST

BALL-FLIGHT MISS: (+)

FLIGHT DESCRIPTION: Excessively high and short iron shots or popped-up shots when a ball is teed up and struck with a driver or fairway wood. Usually ball has too much backspin.

IMPACT CONDITION: Deep divots with irons off the ground. Marks on the top part of the face or the top of woods when the ball is teed up. Also look for broken tees and a possible divot.

CAUSE OF MISS: A swing that's too steep/narrow.

ONE-FIX GOLFER: Incorporate one (-) element from the swing charts in this order of priority: downswing, backswing, impact/follow-through, and address. Note: If your ball-flight miss changes to a (-) category, go to the instructions for the two-fix golfer.

RECOMMENDATIONS FOR THE ONE-FIX GOLFER: Downswing: thrust right hip at ball while restricting shoulder turn. Backswing: swing arms, club flatter; or make bigger shoulder, hip turn. Impact/follow-through: swing arms, club more in-to-out to right of target line; or restrict shoul-

der, hip turn to left; or hit more up at the ball. Address:
stand farther away from ball.

TWO-FIX GOLFER: First incorporate a (-) element from either the downswing or impact/follow-through chart, and
then, if your shots don't dramatically improve after some
practice, incorporate a (+) element from either the address
or backswing chart.

RECOMMENDATIONS FOR THE TWO-FIX GOLFER: Fix No.
1—Downswing: let hips slide toward target and upper
body tilt away from it; or thrust right hip at the ball while
restricting shoulder turn. Impact/follow-through: keep
some weight on right leg and allow lower body to finish
closer to target than upper body; or hit more up at the ball.
Fix. No. 2—Address: bend spine over more. Backswing:
make steeper shoulder turn; or point shaft more to right at
top (across the line).

The other shot that flies too high is what I call the "high-
shallow." This ball-flight miss is almost always produced with
short, high-lofted irons, but the remedy for it is the same as
the "low-shallow" from Chapter Nine. The high-shallow is the
product of a very shallow/wide (-) approach, which slides the
bottom of the clubface under the ball. The ball then rolls up
the high-lofted face and is popped up in the air. In rare cases,
you might see a high-shallow miss with a lower-lofted club,
but only when the ball is sitting up in the rough or on a tee.
To verify this miss, your impact condition with an iron will
typically be no divot or a very shallow one behind the ball.

The high-shallow ball-flight miss mostly falls into the
one-fix category, but in rare cases, two fixes are required. Remember, the fault causing this ball flight is a shallow/wide
impact (-). If your swing is in the one-fix category, then sim-

ply incorporating a (+) element will neutralize the problem and give you a more penetrating flight. Sometimes, however, the shallow/wide impact (-) is an overreaction to a swing that has too many (+) elements. In that case, you're a two-fix candidate.

To fix a low-shallow miss, I'd recommend incorporating one of these elements in the chart order I prescribe:

- **DURING THE DOWNSWING:** 1. Shift your body weight onto your left leg; 2. Swing your arms and club more left, toward an out-to-in path.
- **DURING THE BACKSWING:** 1. Make a steeper shoulder turn; 2. Increase your spine angle by lowering it; 3. Make a more upright arm and club swing.
- **DURING THE IMPACT/FOLLOW-THROUGH:** 1. Swing more down at the ball; 2. Make a bigger shoulder and hip turn around to the left. 3. Lean the shaft forward so the top end is closer to the target than the clubhead. At address: Bend your spine over more.

If your ball-flight miss changes to a (+) after you incorporate one of these (+) elements, then you'll know your swing is in the two-fix category.

With a two-fix golfer, the top of the backswing is actually too steep/narrow (+), and the (-) impact and resulting high-shallow miss is because of a compensation move that occurs in the second half of the swing. Just like all two-fix golfers, what you need to do is to first identify the half of your swing where the major (+) element resides and neutralize it by incorporating a (-) element. In this case, you know the (+) is in the first half, because your ball flight is always the same as the large element in the second half. Since a low-shallow is a

(-), that means the second half of the swing is also (-). Thus, the (+) is in the first half.

You should first incorporate a (-) element into your address or backswing. You've got a lot of elements to choose from, but I have some recommendations:

- **AT ADDRESS:** Tilt your spine more to the right and put more weight on your right leg.
- **DURING THE BACKSWING:** 1. Make a flatter shoulder turn; 2. Make a flatter arm and club swing; 3. Make a bigger shoulder and hip turn.

Unfortunately, after incorporating that (-), you will probably start hitting tops or whiffs, both of which are extremely (-) ball-flight misses. Nevertheless, keep practicing the new fix in the first half of the swing and see if you don't intuitively correct the downswing issue. If you keep hitting whiffs and tops, however, you will need to incorporate a (+) element in the second half of your swing to neutralize that (-) compensation. Here is what I would prescribe:

- **DURING THE DOWNSWING:** 1. Get your entire body moving more toward the target and onto your left leg; 2. Close the clubface.
- **DURING IMPACT/FOLLOW-THROUGH:** 1. Get your upper body to finish directly over your lower body with all your weight on your left leg; 2. Lean the shaft forward and hit more down on the ball.

Again, these recommendations might not work for you as well as other elements in the charts, so feel free to experiment until you find the right adjustments.

HIGH-SHALLOW CHECKLIST

BALL-FLIGHT MISS: (-)

FLIGHT DESCRIPTION: Shot that balloons nearly straight up in the air, usually with high-lofted irons or lower-lofted clubs when the ball is teed up.

IMPACT CONDITION: Shallow divot behind the ball, or none at all.

CAUSE OF MISS: Too-shallow approach, and the ball is struck on the upswing.

ONE-FIX GOLFER: Incorporate one (+) element from the swing charts in this order of priority: downswing, backswing, impact/follow-through, and address. Note: If your ball-flight miss changes to a (+) category, go to the instructions for the two-fix golfer.

RECOMMENDATIONS FOR THE ONE-FIX GOLFER: Downswing: shift body weight onto left leg; or swing arms, club more left, toward an out-to-in path. Backswing: make steeper shoulder turn; or increase spine angle by lowering it; or make more upright arm, club swing. Impact/follow-through: swing more down at ball; or make a bigger shoulder, hip turn around to the left; or lean the shaft forward so the top end is closer to the target than the clubhead. Address: bend your spine over more.

TWO-FIX GOLFER: First incorporate a (-) element from the address or backswing chart and then, if flight doesn't dramatically improve with some practice, incorporate a (+) element from the downswing or impact/follow-through charts.

RECOMMENDATIONS FOR THE TWO-FIX GOLFER: Fix No. 1—Address: tilt spine more to right and put more weight on right leg. Backswing: make flatter shoulder turn; or make flatter arm, club swing; or make bigger shoulder, hip turn. Fix No. 2—Downswing: move entire body more toward the target and onto left leg; or close clubface. Impact/follow-through: finish with upper body directly over lower body, 100 percent weight on left leg; or lean shaft forward; or hit more down on ball.

Chapter Eleven

FINAL THOUGHTS

L et me start this chapter by saying that now that you've learned the system, I hope you realize you possess the knowledge to enjoy this sport for a lifetime. This book is the single greatest piece of golf equipment you own. Not only will it help you fix your swing right now, but it will also give you the blueprint you need to always understand what's happening with your shots and your swing and to fix things whenever they go awry.

I bring this up because I don't want to give you the wrong impression. This book will assuredly help fix your swing—right now. But the nature of this game is that things might not always be so rosy. Playing good golf for a long period of time is possible, but I compare it to steering a boat in a rough sea toward a distant lighthouse. If you just take a bearing on the lighthouse and hold steady to that compass heading, the wind and currents will move you way off course. I sure hope the coast guard eventually finds you. What you should have done on your journey toward that lighthouse is to make a near-constant series of adjustments. You steer a little right, then left, more left, oops, back to the right, hold steady . . . steady . . . now hard left! It's the same as your journey in golf: You'll get it and then lose it, get it again and hope you can keep it, and then it's gone again. That's the hard truth. But when your swing starts to slip away, the knowledge you've learned from this book will help you know precisely which way it's slipping and exactly how to get it back. You'll get your boat back on course before it wrecks on the shoals.

Any time you get into a rut and are hitting bad shots, you'll now understand immediately which category of misses your swing is producing—a (+) or a (-). In the past, you've probably hit shots that have gone left and right and you were bewildered. We call that "Army golf"—you know, left, right, left, right. . . . You might have told your golf buddies that you had "a bunch of different swings out there today." You hit pushes and hooks, you hit some fat and some thin, and you couldn't get your fairway woods up in the air and couldn't get your wedges out of the air. You might have thought that your game was hopeless and then gone in search of the nearest golf pro to completely overhaul your swing.

But now, with the help of this book, that doesn't have to happen. Instead, I want you to realize that, even though you were spraying it all over the course, all those different ball flights that you named are from the same category. They are all (-) misses. You will be able to recognize that and know that the cause of all those bad shots was a swing that was too (-). If this happens again, you'll know you're only one or two (+) adjustments away from correcting your problem. It's the same as if you had a round or two where all you did was hit slices, pulls, and steep-tops. Don't think you have to revamp your swing. Know that you only have to incorporate one or two (-) elements into your swing to start hitting solid shots with a reliable ball flight.

Understand that part of the game is managing your expectations, and realize that nobody delivers the club to the ball perfectly every time. So don't get upset, frustrated, or desperate when your swing goes awry from time to time. Accept it, fix it, and move on.

Speaking of fixing it, I'm sure many of you are cringing at the prospects of going through a two-fix golfer's process, since it's more daunting than a one-fix golfer's process. Well, with this book, you only have to experience it once. After you straighten out a two-fix situation, the next time things drift off course, you can one-fix the problem before the mistake gets so large that you start to make a compensation error in your swing. Those large watermelons you had to juggle the first time around can be gone for good if you stay on top of things. Correct the error when it's still just a lemon, and as the saying goes, turn it into lemonade.

Want more good news? The system also can be used to improve your short-game shots. Some examples: If you aren't taking any divot or only a slight divot behind the ball, then your chipping or pitching swing is too shallow (-). Ever blade a pitch or chip shot? Your swing is also too shallow. Meanwhile, if your divots are chunky, then you're too steep (+). Taking the application of the plus/minus system to the short game a step further, the test for determining whether your swing needs one fix or two also remains the same. If your problem swings over to the opposite side of the charts after you incorporate an element to fix your too (+) or too (-) chip or pitch, then you know you're a two-fix golfer.

Here's an example: You might be too shallow (-) at impact because you're picking the club straight up in the air with a very steep/narrow backswing (+), and then, to avoid burying the wedge in the ground, compensating in the downswing by swinging up on the ball (-). If this is you, you're in the two-fix category. What you should do is first neutralize the (+) problem in the first half of the swing—the steep/narrow takeaway—by incorporating a (-). Then you have to deal with the compensation move—swinging up on the ball—by incorporating a (+). As you can see, the process stays the same, so pay attention to your divots when you chip and pitch and you'll be able to correct issues just like you can with your full swing.

Again, there will be times when you're hitting short-game and full-swing shots great, and times when things go south. But remember the goal. It's the genesis of this book. I want you hitting shots that are both solid *and* predictable. It's that second part that might give you pause. After all, I just got done saying that your swing likely will go awry from time to time. So if that's a common occurrence, then how can you play with a reliable ball flight?

The answer is simple: Stick with your swing and your style. Every swing and style when neutral will produce a reliable shot pattern that suits that golfer's DNA. Nicklaus's pattern when neutral was high fades, Trevino's was low fades, Watson's was high hooks, Player's was low hooks. I'm sure Trevino or Player must have at some point thought, "Wouldn't it be nice to hit that high shot like Jack?" But they instinctively knew that it did not fit their style and to change their style would have been totally wrong. Instead, they played their shot pattern, let Jack play his, and the game was on. That's the secret: Play your style's predictable shot pattern. That's the way to be solid and predictable with a correct, repetitive impact. The more you work on trying to fix and refine your style to produce solid shots, the more predictable your ball flight will become and the better chance you'll have at success. If you stick with your swing and style, each time a problem occurs, you'll be able to solve it more quickly and easily than the previous time. Think of it like this: You'll be a master mechanic of your own car. Sure, you know the engine will overheat and the steering will get knocked out of alignment from time to time, but you have the tools to quickly repair the problem. The quicker you repair it and get back to your swing, the more reliable your ball flight will become.

This is a lesson that all of us should remember—even the pros. While some of today's very best golfers have tried to repeatedly overhaul their swings (I'm sure one player immediately comes to mind), I believe this is a mistake. Jack Nicklaus stuck with his natural swing his entire career. So did Lee Trevino and Billy Casper. Ben Hogan never changed his style; he just continued to fix it and refine it. Jim Furyk is perhaps the best modern example of an elite golfer who hasn't changed. I'm not saying golfers can't be successful if they try a complete swing change; it's just that more often than not it doesn't work, even after a tremendous amount of effort. Nick Faldo is a notable exception; when he underwent his first big change, it worked and he became a great champion. It also worked for Peter Jacobsen and Don Pooley. Both had better careers after the change than before. But it doesn't pay off for the vast majority. Golf's scrap heap is full of players who lost their way by getting away from what was natural.

Remember, once you've developed your own swing and are hitting neutral shots that you can easily repeat, all you have to do is make simple fixes when things go bad. And even in the rare instances when you do find your swing in a bigger mess, just remember that there are only two kinds of golfers in the world: the golfer who needs only one fix and the golfer who needs two fixes. That doesn't sound so bad, does it?

Finally—and please remember this—don't mess with a good thing. Any time you're playing solid and predictable golf and you start messing with your swing because you read some golf tip or because someone gave you advice to hit it better, remember that when you try it, it will automatically make your impact more (+) or (-). You're guaranteed to go from neutral to either (+) or (-). The only way that the element you incorporate is going to produce a neutral ball flight is if you also incorporate an element from the other side of the charts to balance it out. Any changes to a neutral swing must introduce both a (+) and a (-). You have to do it in twos.

I'm warning you about tinkering with your swing because it's exactly the same advice I got from some of the great veterans when I first came onto the PGA Tour in 1968. Back then, a lot of the pros were called "rabbits" not just because we had to qualify on Mondays, but also because we had rabbit ears and would listen to any and all advice. We all thought that we were only one tip from beating Jack and Arnie. I can still recall the guys who came on tour with pretty good games and left in a shambles because they began tinkering and tinkering with their swings and eventually lost their way. So again, please stick to what you know works.

Now you know all of my secrets. My first two books were about the issues of swing shape. All swings are either one- or two-plane. The best swing in the world is one or the other, and so is the worst. But this book is about knowing how to fix your one-plane or two-plane swing using the simple plus/minus formula. I want you to own your golf swing, understand your DNA, and be able to correct your problem as quickly as your next shot. It reminds me of something tour pro Matt Kuchar said when asked about swing changes he made to suddenly become one of the best golfers on the PGA Tour. At the time, he was working with my good friend Chris O'Connell (I founded my company, Plane Truth Golf, with Chris and a very talented amateur golfer named Mike Crisanti). Matt was asked how long it took him to get used to his new swing. "Exactly five swings," Kuchar replied. And he wasn't joking.

"Jim Hardy is the kind of mastermind behind it," Kuchar said. "I think their theory is, listen, if within ten golf balls you're not hitting it better with whatever they've told you to do, then it's not the right ingredient. If they plug in the right ingredient, it might feel awkward at first, but when the golf ball is hitting the center of the club and it's going where you want it to go, you go, 'I can do this.'"

So when I say you can correct your problem on the very next shot, I'm not exaggerating. Sure, it will probably take some time to get used to anything new you incorporate into a swing, but the prospect that it could happen so fast, I hope, is exciting.

With the help of Chris and Mike, I'm now in the process of training and certifying hundreds of instructors in several countries on how to use the plus/minus system for their students. The goal is to get these instructors to understand that this is truly the only effective way to teach the game to anyone who walks in for a lesson. I can say this because we've studied virtually every swing theory and instruction method we've come across. Some theories and methods are great and are working for a large number of players, but it always seems like someone is left behind. Not with this system. We've studied all kinds of ways to hit solid shots with a repeatable ball flight, and in every case, the reason it worked was because the pluses and minuses balanced. Whether it was Jim Furyk, Bubba Watson, or some guy who just won his third straight club championship, the result was always the same.

Our certified instructors know that if that club champion with a strange-looking swing comes to them for a lesson, they don't overhaul his or her swing. They just work within that golfer's style and get that swing back to neutral. They know it's the key to that golfer's success.

I started this book by saying that I believe all golf swings are either one- or two-plane. That's your basic style. But within those categories, you've got many, many variations of swings that not only work, but might belong to a golfer in the Hall of Fame. If you want to get there someday, or simply want to beat your buddies in your next Saturday morning Nassau, don't let anyone talk you out of your swing. Fix it and refine it.

ACKNOWLEDGMENTS

I first want to thank Bill Shinker, the publisher of Gotham Books, for recognizing and believing that the plus/minus swing DNA concept is such a revolutionary notion. His leadership and the hard work at Gotham of editor Travers Johnson and copy editor Gary Perkinson, whose ideas were invaluable, made *Solid Contact* possible. I also want to thank my literary agent, Farley Chase of the Waxman Agency in New York City, for his work and friendship in shepherding me through three books and his attentions to all my questions and requests.

I first publicly introduced the plus/minus system at the PGA of America International Teaching and Coaching Summit in Nashville in 1990. I continued to refine it over the years, and it has become not only the bedrock of my teaching but also the foundation of my instructor certification programs. I had always presented the concept in an oral form. And when many people encouraged me to write a book on the subject, I thought it would be an easy task. That notion couldn't have been further from the truth. The problem was that when I presented the system in the past, it was always taught to experienced instructors—not average golfers. If I was going to do a book on the subject, it would have to be technically sophisticated enough that teachers could use it like a textbook, but also simple enough that average golfers could understand it and use the book without an instructor. The concept is simple. But explaining it to golfers of every skill level is very difficult. Ron Kaspriske was my key to accomplishing that. He pushed and pounded my ideas, constantly forming them into text that is understandable, practical, and functional for all golfers—from tour players and professional instructors to high-handicappers. I am so thankful to him for all his hard work and guidance. And especially his patience.

I wish to thank Scott Addison for his innovative work in creating the pencil-sketch type drawings that add so much to this book. Thanks also to my associate, Chris O'Connell, who posed for all the photos that Addison used for his illustrations.

My appreciation also goes to Mike LaBauve, who has always considered the plus/minus system my greatest contribution to golf instruction and has encouraged professionals and amateurs to learn the system and apply it. For many years, his support has been a great encouragement to me.

I thank my dear wife, Marilyn, who has been the test subject for all my ideas. She has willfully undertaken my best and worst so I could see them in action firsthand.

Finally, my profound gratitude goes to Chris O'Connell and Mike Crisanti, who have formed Plane Truth Golf with me and who are the driving force of our endeavors. Without them, I would have accomplished far less with my life's work. They are incredibly talented men and the dearest of friends. Thank you for all you are and all you do.

ABOUT THE AUTHORS

JIM HARDY

Perhaps the truest compliment a physician can get is when another doctor comes in for a checkup. In a sense, that's who Jim Hardy is to the golf-instruction community. Teachers all around the world come to seminars conducted by Hardy to hear his original thoughts on the golf swing. It's a knowledge built from forty-four years around the game, a career that has included playing on the PGA and Champions Tours, designing and managing golf courses, and conducting tireless research on swing mechanics.

Hardy was named the National PGA Teacher of the Year in 2007, is a member of the Texas Golf Hall of Fame, has been nominated to the teacher's division of the World Golf Hall of Fame, is ranked in the top 10 on *Golf Digest*'s list of America's 50 Greatest Teachers, and has been on the biannual rankings list for more than two decades. And for more than twenty-five years, he also has been on *Golf Magazine*'s "Top 100 Teachers in America" list.

Perhaps the thing that Jim is most well-known for is his revolutionary concept that all golf swings are either on one plane or two planes. Years of research on this subject prompted him to write the best-selling instruction book *The Plane Truth for Golfers* in 2005. In the years after its debut, "one-plane" and "two-plane" became household phrases for golfers. Both professionals and amateurs embraced the concept, and the book's success spawned a hugely popular DVD series and a second book, *The Plane Truth for Golfers: Master Class.*

A native of Hutchinson, Kansas, Hardy earned All-American honors in 1966 at Oklahoma State University, and then competed on the PGA Tour full-time from 1968 until March 1974. When his playing career ended, Hardy immediately dove into instruction. Among his students have been Frank Beard, Dave Stockton, Carol Mann, Donna Caponi, Hollis Stacy, Brad Faxon, and Mark O'Meara. He currently teaches PGA Tour and Champions Tour professionals Peter Jacobsen, Scott McCarron, Tom Pernice, Bob Tway, Olin Browne, Duffy Waldorf, Chris Tidland, Joe Ogilvie, Scott Piercy, Don Pooley, David Eger, Morris Hatalsky, Mitch Adcock, and Graham Marsh. Among the nationally recognized golf instructors who have studied under Jim are Hank Haney, Mike and Sandy LaBauve, Jim Murphy, Laird Small, Martin Hall, Roger Gunn, Paul Gorman, Chris O'Connell, Krista Dunton, Cindy Ferrell, Marty Fleckman, E. J. Pfister, Carol Mann, and Rick Sellers.

In the spring of 2009, Hardy, who has been conducting teaching/playing seminars for golf professionals for seven years, launched a new instructor certification program. In addition, he unveiled an interactive instructional website—the first of its kind—designed to support instructors with the solutions to any ball-flight or swing-shape fault their students might have.

Hardy lives in the Houston area with his wife, Marilyn,

who is a plus-2 handicap and who has competed in local, state, and national tournaments, including two U.S. Women's Opens. His daughter, Rachel, 14, is a multisport athlete and an excellent junior golfer. For additional information, please visit planetruthgolf.com.

RON KASPRISKE

Ron Kaspriske has been an editor and writer for *Golf Digest* for more than a decade and has been writing about golf instruction for more than fifteen years. In 2009, his section of the magazine—"The Digest"—was nominated by the American Society of Magazine Editors as one of the five best in publishing. He's also won four writing awards from the Golf Writers Association of America and was the Southwest Florida PGA's 1997 Amateur of the Year for his contributions to golf. He has two previously published books about the game and works closely with many of its biggest players and teachers when they contribute to the magazine. A Florida native and a graduate of the University of Florida, Kaspriske resides in Norwalk, Connecticut.